How To Know

THE

WESTERN

TREES

How To Know

THE
WESTERN
TREES

Harry J. Baerg

SECOND EDITION

WM. C. BROWN COMPANY PUBLISHERS
Dubuque, Iowa

Library of Congress Catalog Card Number: 78-167735

ISBN 0—697—04801—2 (Cloth)
ISBN 0—697—04800—4 (Paper)

THE PICTURED-KEY NATURE SERIES

How To Know The—

AQUATIC PLANTS, Prescott, 1969
BEETLES, Jaques, 1951
BUTTERFLIES, Ehrlich, 1961
CACTI, Dawson, 1963
EASTERN LAND SNAILS, Burch, 1962
ECONOMIC PLANTS, Jaques, 1948, 1958
FALL FLOWERS, Cuthbert, 1948
FRESHWATER ALGAE, Prescott, 1954, 1970
FRESHWATER FISHES, Eddy, 1957, 1969
GRASSES, Pohl, 1953, 1968
GRASSHOPPERS, Helfer, 1963
IMMATURE INSECTS, Chu, 1949
INSECTS, Jaques, 1947
LAND BIRDS, Jaques, 1947
LICHENS, Hale, 1969
LIVING THINGS, Jaques, 1946
MAMMALS, Booth, 1949
MARINE ISOPOD CRUSTACEANS, Schultz, 1969
MOSSES AND LIVERWORTS, Conard, 1944, 1956
PLANT FAMILIES, Jaques, 1948
POLLEN AND SPORES, Kapp, 1969
PROTOZOA, Jahn, 1949
ROCKS AND MINERALS, Helfer, 1970
SEAWEEDS, Dawson, 1956
SPIDERS, Kaston, 1952
SPRING FLOWERS, Cuthbert, 1943, 1949
TAPEWORMS, Schmidt, 1970
TREMATODES, Schell, 1970
TREES, Jaques, 1946
WATER BIRDS, Jaques-Ollivier, 1960
WEEDS, Jaques, 1959
WESTERN TREES, Baerg, 1955

Printed in United States of America

PREFACE

HE mountainous regions including the Rockies and westward which are covered by this book contain some of the largest timber reserves of the nation. In them the conifers predominate. The hardwoods of the eastern and southern states are largely lacking though there are numbers of oaks, birches, maples and semi-hardwoods in some localities. Fortunately wood does not have to be hard to be useful.

The great stands of Douglas-fir, pine and spruce provide large quantities of building lumber and veneer; the cedars are made into millions of telephone and power line poles as well as shingles for roofing; the hemlock and spruces supply the pulp from which the paper is made for the presses and packaging businesses of the country. The railways of much of the country are laid on ties of western larch and fir, and the farms are fenced with cedar and tamarack posts.

There are giants in the land. The redwoods, sequoias and Douglas-firs are among the largest trees to be found on the continent. The bristlecone pines of California have the distinction of being the oldest living things. They go back in time beyond the building of the pyramids or the existence of the Chaldean civilization.

Climate changes from the arctic tundras of northern Alaska to semi-tropical regions of southern California, and from the abnormally heavy rainfall of the British Columbia-Washington coastline to the extreme aridity of the deserts of Nevada and Arizona not only provide a habitat for a large variety of different species, but also produce a great variation within the species.

In the plan of this book we have tried to include all the native western trees found in the area included on our map together with the more popular introduced trees and common fruit trees. Shrubs have been excluded. Certain genera of plants are trees in some species and shrubs in others. We have tried, as far as possible, to make accurate distinctions. Some species are shrubs in some localities but attain tree characteristics in ideal environment. Such are generally included. The United States Department of Agriculture Check List has been used as a guide in this. We have described 383 trees in this book and pictured 247 of them.

Of necessity a number of standard works covering this field or certain portions of it have been referred to in making up this book.

v

In addition to this the author wishes to acknowledge the assistance and encouragement given him by Dr. E. S. Booth of Anacortes, Washington, the reading and checking of proofs by James Grant of the Canadian Forest Entomology branch at Vernon and the help in preparation of the manuscript given by his wife, Ida May Baerg.

The drawings are the author's work. They attempt to show the main distinguishing characteristics of the various trees and also the general locality in which they are found. The range can be only approximate because of the size of the maps and the meager knowledge available on some species. Information on certain rare trees is scarce, but great care has been taken to make this work as reliable and informative as possible. We hope the readers will find it so.

We have tried to keep the terminology simple enough for use in high school as well as college classes. The hobbyist also who wishes to learn more about trees should find it equally usable.

Harry J. Baerg.

HARRY J. BAERG,
Takoma Park, Maryland

CONTENTS

HOW TO KNOW TREES

DUCATION consists of a distinction of differences." These words coming from the lips of a respected college professor of mine contain truth that we can apply to our study of trees. What makes trees different from other plants? A common answer would be, "They are taller." Such a generalization naturally has exceptions. Some mature trees are hardly five feet in height while herbs and grasses like Teasel or Sorghum grow from six to ten feet tall.

If we say, "Trees have woody stems and remain erect after a frost while herbs die down," we are progressing in our definition. But what about shrubs? We are faced with the need for another distinction. "Trees have one main stem coming from the rootstock while shrubs have several."

Our definition then would probably be, "A tree is a tall, woody, perennial plant with one main stem rising out of its root system."

In trying to distinguish differences among trees themselves we find that some of them retain their leaves during the winter, others shed them. In general we find that the cone-bearing, or coniferous, trees retain their leaves. We sometimes call them evergreens. A notable exception to this rule is the larch or tamarack group.

The broad-leaved trees generally shed their foliage in the fall; we refer to them as "deciduous." There are several exceptions to this, especially among the southern trees. Examples are the live oaks, laurels, arbutus and eucalyptus.

Among the broad-leaved and coniferous trees again there are other divisions that are used in distinguishing between still smaller groups of trees. All are made use of in learning to know trees.

One need not be a professional botanist in order to study trees and acquire useful information concerning them. A beginner will do well to become acquainted first with the trees in his own yard or street and then go farther afield, continually broadening his knowledge and never ceasing to look for new varieties

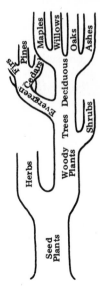

Figure 1

1

or new facts concerning old ones. He may think he has found all the species in his part of the country, but a trip up a nearby mountain may show him several new ones on different altitude levels. He will find that each tree has its favorite habitat, and he will soon learn to expect and find certain trees in certain places. If he is not careful he may even discover some day that he is an authority on trees in his locality.

There is a strange sort of tree blindness that may afflict a person at times. I remember searching for a specimen of spruce tree in the neighborhood where I once lived and not finding any till a neighbor pointed one out to me. I was familiar with spruce trees but had not been able to see this one till I was shown. After that I saw quite a number of them, some right near the house. Then one day I saw two Ponderosa pines among the fir and white pine along the road. I was well acquainted with them from another locality, but had not seen these though I passed them and worked near them for nearly a year. They are still the only ones I know in that locality. You may think you know all the trees in your neighborhood and then suddenly find a new one that has been there all along.

LIFE AND GROWTH OF A TREE

A young tree has branches close to the ground. On older trees the first branches are sometimes as much as fifty to one hundred feet from the ground. Superficial observers are apt to jump to the conclusion that the lowest branches of a tree are the first ones it has had, and that the section of the tree between them and the ground has stretched during growth.

I remember a certain tall-story artist in my youth regaling his gullible audience with a tale of building a house on a large stump on the west coast. According to this prevaricator it had to be abandoned after a few years because the upward growth of the stump necessitated a longer ladder to the front door each year.

Actually the trunk of a tree does not stretch upward. No, not even in rubber trees! The only part of the tree that expands in length is the growth section of the current year at the tips of the twigs or roots. The lower branches of the tree die (Fig. 3), usually for lack of sunlight, and are broken off by the expanding of the thickness of the trunk. Between

Figure 2

the bark and the wood of last year's growth is the *cambium layer*. Here the growth of the trunk takes place (Fig. 4). Food from the leaves comes down with the sap on its way to the root system and the cells are fed along the way. They multiply and develop into what is known as a "growth ring." From these concentric rings in the cross-section of a tree its age and history can be determined.

Figure 3

A similar but more minute addition is made on the inside bark next to the wood. The combined expansion of both wood and inner bark causes the outside bark to pull apart forming ribs, furrows, interlaced fibers, scales or plates. On some trees like the sycamore it peels off and is shed in flakes. The many different bark surfaces thus formed in growth are valuable aids in knowing different species. Smooth bark shows lenticels, or pores for breathing. (Fig. 5)

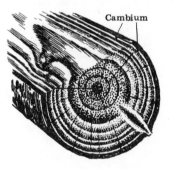

Cambium

Figure 4

In the leaves of a tree the water sent up by the roots is combined with carbon dioxide from the air in the presence of sunlight to form sugar which is the food of the tree. This sugar could not be made were it not for the presence, in the leaves, of a substance called, *"chlorophyll"* which acts as a working agent. Chlorophyll is green in color and is present in all but the parasitic plants. That is the reason why green is such a common color among plants. The leaves are the food factory of the plant. Some plants that have no leaves have green twigs which do the work performed by the leaves in most plants.

Figure 5. Species may be often recognized by their bark.

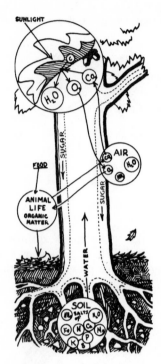

Figure 6. How trees get their food and grow.

During the day the leaves are able to manufacture more sugar than the sap is able to carry away. This excess is changed to starch which is insoluble. Then at night it is changed back into sugar and dissolved by the sap to be carried to the different parts of the tree. Plants also store food as protein and fat.

During the process of sugar making, which is known as *"photosynthesis,"* much water and oxygen is given off. This goes out through the same openings that let in the carbon dioxide. They are found on the under side of the leaf and can be opened and closed. These openings, called *"stomata,"* are closed at night because photosynthesis takes place only in daylight hours.

In winter when most trees are dormant and the ground often frozen this loss of water through the leaves would be hard for the roots to replace. To prevent dehydration the trees shed their leaves. Those species that do not do so have thick waxcovered leaves that lose little moisture when the stomata are closed.

In the illustration (Fig. 7) several types of leaf shapes are shown that are likely to be found in the west and the names that will be used in connection with them in this book. On a leaf the flat part is known as the blade and the stem part as the *petiole*.

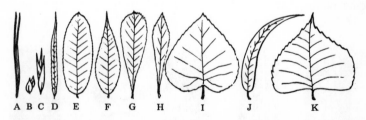

Figure 7. A. needle-like; B. scale-like; C. awl-like; D. linear; E. oblong; F. lanceolate; G. oblanceolate; H. spatulate; I. cordate; J. sickle-shaped; K. deltoid.

Leaves that have no petioles are called *sessile leaves*. At the base of the petiole there will often be found two small leaflets, these are referred to as the *stipules* (Fig. 8). All that appears beyond the bud at the juncture of the petiole and the twig is the leaf. This is important to remember for sometimes several *leaflets* grow out of one petiole and a beginner may become confused and consider each one as a leaf when in reality the whole thing is the leaf. Such a group of leaflets on one petiole are known as *compound leaves*. The illustration shows two types; the *pinnate* where the leaflets are attached at the side and end of the petiole, and the *palmate* where they all radiate from the end of the petiole. (Fig. 9)

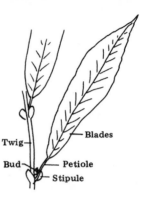

Figure 8

Leaf veins may also be arranged in similar patterns and are referred to by the same names. (Fig. 10) Leaf surfaces may be smooth or hairy.

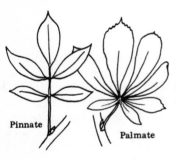

Figure 9

The edges of leaves come in a great variety of patterns from the entire or smooth to the parted where the cleft goes right to the main vein producing a compound leaf. The names of the different ones are shown in the accompanying illustration. (Fig. 11) The shape of the base and of the apex of a leaf offer characters for identification. (Fig. 12)

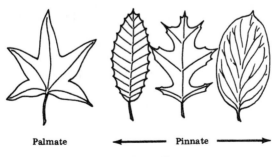

Palmate ◄———— Pinnate ————►

Figure 10

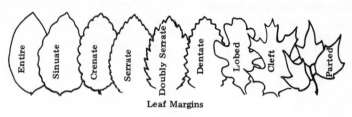

Leaf Margins

Figure 11

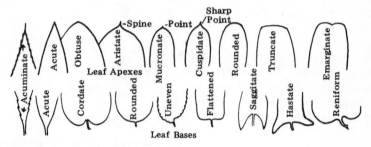

Leaf Bases

Figure 12

Needles of coniferous trees can be an interesting study. We find that some grow singly on the sides and ends of twigs, others grow in bundles. Of the latter we find that the bundles consist of 2, 3, 4, 5, or even larger numbers according to the species of tree to which they belong. The cross sections of the needles correspond to the number in the bundle. One of two needles is half a circle, one of three needles is one third of a circle and so on. (Fig. 13)

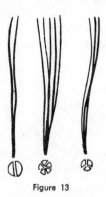

Figure 13

The twig of a tree is interesting and useful especially in identifying trees in winter. Not only for types of leaf scars that may be found but also for the type of pith formation revealed by longitudinal or cross sections. Thorns are usually modified twigs. Spines and barbs are found in many different parts of plants, especially in desert varieties. Sometimes leaves have spines on them as in the holly, seed coverings often do, and twigs still more often.

The juncture of the leaf and twig is spoken of as the *"node."* Some leaves are attached on opposite sides of twigs, some are *alternate,* some *whorled* and some *spiral.* (Fig. 14)

In our tree descriptions in this book we have presumed that all trees have flowers. Strictly speaking this is not true, for only the angiosperms have that distinction. It is only for convenience in naming that we have referred to sex organs of the conifers as flowers. These trees have staminate and pistillate cones which take the place of flowers. For simplicity and brevity we

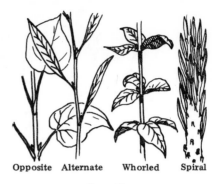

Opposite   Alternate   Whorled   Spiral

Figure 14

have referred to the two types as male and female instead of staminate and pistillate.

Flowers vary greatly in trees. On some, like the horse chestnuts and catalpas, they are large and showy. On others they are small and inconspicuous. A complete flower has *calyx, corolla, stamens* and *pistil*. You will find these parts shown on the diagram. (Fig. 15) Flowers are also classified as *perfect* and *imperfect*. A perfect flower need have only stamens and pistil. If it has only stamens or only pistil, it is an imperfect flower. In that case it may either be that there are staminate and pistillate flowers on the same tree or it may be that one tree bears only staminate flowers (a male tree), and another has all pistillate flowers (a female tree). When trees have both

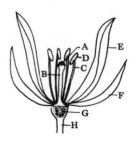

Figure 15. AB. pistil; A. stigma; B. style; CD. stamen; C. filament; D. anther; E. petal (making a corolla); F. sepal (making the calyx); G. ovary; H. pedicel.

flowers on one tree they are spoken of as *monoecious,* when they have one kind on one tree and one kind on another they are called *dioecious.* (Fig. 16)

Date palms are dioecious and a date grower will plant only a few staminate palms in his orchard, all the rest being pistillate or

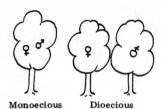

Monoecious   Dioecious

Figure 16

the equivalent of female. At blossom time he artificially pollinates the females with pollen from the male blossoms. In this way he avoids cluttering up his orchard with male trees that would bear no dates.

Flower grouping is another way in which kinds of trees vary, and for that reason it can be a help in identifying different ones. Several different types of flower clusters are shown and named here. (Fig. 17)

TYPES OF FLOWERS

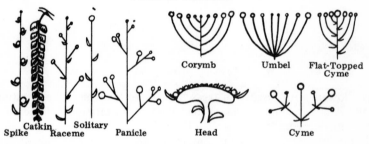

Figure 17

"By their fruits ye shall know them" applies very well to trees. Fruits are more important than flowers in this respect because in most cases they are larger and more easily seen, and because they remain on the tree longer. Of course we cannot always tell by the fruit because some trees (the males) do not bear fruit, some bear only in alternate years and most of them do not bear until they have reached a certain stage of maturity. Since trees do not die annually it is not important for them to bear seed every year. Some of the pines, the Lodgepole for one, bear two different kinds of cones. One disperses its seeds as it ripens, the other one remains tightly closed for years and does not open to seed out till after a forest fire has passed through. Then a forest of pines comes up as a cover crop for large and slower growing trees.

Several different types of seed structure are indicated in the diagram. (Fig. 18)

Conifers, poplars, willows and other wind-pollinated trees produce large quantities of pollen to make sure that some of it will reach the right place. In order to fertilize the egg of the female flower it is necessary for at least one grain of pollen to catch on the sticky head of the pistil which is called the stigma. From here it grows down the style to the ovary

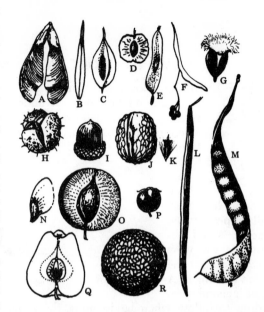

Figure 18. Fruits. A-F. samaras, maple, ash, buckwheat-tree, elm, ailanthus. basswood; G. capsule, cottonwood; H. prickly husk, horsechestnut; I. acorn, oak; J. nut, walnut; K. achene, syracuse; L. capsule, catalpa; M. pod, locust; N. winged seed, pine; O. drupe, prune; P. pome, serviceberry; Q. pome, apple; R. compound fruit, Osage orange.

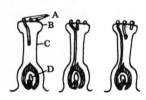

Figure 19

which it enters. (Fig. 19) The fertilized ovule becomes a seed.

Bees and other insects play an important part in the pollination of trees other than those just mentioned. Locust and linden trees that produce a large number of nectar-rich flowers are valuable sources of honey for the apiarist. He is wise to plant them near his hives.

HOW TO WORK WITH TREES

E VERY tree lover will want to plant some of his favorite trees around his home. It adds immeasurably to the sense of permanence even if one is not possessed with a sentimental nostalgia for the "shade of the old apple tree."

In planting trees around the house it is well to keep in mind how they will appear when mature. Avoid obstructing the view or shading the house too much. A good general pro-

Figure 20

cedure to follow when landscaping the small lot is: to have an open lawn between the house and the street, small trees and shrubs around the house and larger trees in the back yard. The trees like arbor vitae and yew help to break the hard lines of the house and provide a base for it, the large trees behind the house provide a setting for it. (Fig. 20)

When planting any of the poplars or cottonwoods be sure to get cuttings from male trees, otherwise you have rollers of down all over your yard and house in June. Don't break up and destroy the beauty of an open front lawn by planting large, dense-foliage

trees in it. I once had the assignment of removing (one by one at night to avoid giving open offense) a number of such trees from a campus that had been so cluttered by a well meaning soul.

The soil around a new house is usually made up of refuse plaster, left-over gravel, nails, bits of wood, shavings, and paper. This ordinarily does not grow trees to well, so be sure that newly planted trees have good soil about the roots. It is also important that the roots be well spread out in a hole that is large enough. (Fig. 21)

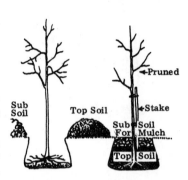

Figure 21

In the natural state most trees propagate from seed. Of the many seeds that fall few, however, become trees. Many seeds never even germinate. For this reason it is better to transplant a small tree than to plant a seed. A number of trees like the willows and poplars can be propagated from cuttings planted in damp earth.

Lombardy poplars in America are all males. When they were first imported from Europe only staminate cuttings were taken and all others have been propagated from them by cuttings. These trees are so much alike because they are all part of the same tree. Since no sexual reproduction has taken place and no seeds have been produced there has been no chance for mutations of genes to produce variations.

Fruit trees, as a rule, will not grow from cuttings, but the orchardists have developed a system of grafting that insures uniform results. Cuttings from a desirable tree are grafted to the one-year-old root stocks of hardy, often wild varieties. (Fig. 22) The resulting trees will have the good characteristics of the tree from which the cuttings came as far as flavor, size, color and shape of the fruit is concerned, but the tree will be hardy and vigorous because of the rootstock it has. To plant an apple orchard from seeds, no matter how good the parent stock, would result in so heterogeneous a mixture of worthless fruit trees as to eliminate the gamble from fruit growing and insure financial loss in spite of the most liberal farm subsidies.

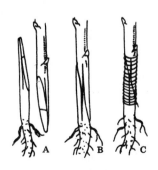

Figure 22

Trees are also changed over from a variety that has become valueless on the market to one that is popular by the process of

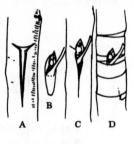

"budding." In this process a bud with part of the bark on it is sliced from a twig of a good variety and slipped into a "T" cut in the bark of one of the branches of the undesirable tree and taped to prevent drying. (Fig. 23) This is done on all the main branches. Then as the grafted buds grow the rest of the limbs are pruned off and only the grafts remain to bear fruit.

Figure 23

PRUNING

On almost any tree whether it is a fruit or shade tree it becomes necessary from time to time to do a little pruning. On shade trees it is often necessary to trim off lower branches or ones that have

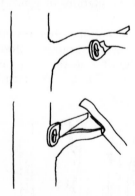

died or have been partly broken. These should be cut close to the trunk and given a coat of lead paint that the tree may have a chance to grow over the wound before the rot of the dead wood enters the trunk. When large branches need to be cut they should first be undercut about six inches from the trunk, then an upper cut can safely be made right next to the trunk without danger of the half cut branch breaking and splitting off a large splint from the trunk. (Fig. 24)

In pruning orchard trees the main objectives are: to let light into the tree, to allow ladder room and, lastly, to build a strong, symmetrical tree. Branches should not rub against each other or fruit will be damaged. Tops often need to be cut down that the fruit may be reached without an extension ladder.

Figure 24

Pruning may be done at any time of the year but the tree suffers least if it is done during the latter part of the dormant season, in early spring before the leaves come out.

A weak crotch in a tree may often be strengthened by twining together two shoots from opposite sides as shown in the illustration. (Fig. 25) They will grow together and make a powerful bond. Large scars and decayed portions should be scraped clean and filled with concrete in such a way that the tree can grow cleanly over it.

Figure 25

One of the most common insect pests on ornamental and orchard trees is the plant aphid. It is carried up the tree by ants and can usually be controlled if ants can be kept off the tree by bands of "tanglefoot" or other means. In orchards a spray of nicotine sulphate is used.

Thousands of different insects live in trees. Some do considerable damage, but in most cases the trees are able to survive without calling in a tree doctor. If birds are encouraged to stay around they will do much to help preserve a healthy balance. Vigorous growth can be induced by mulch and fertilizers and the tree will have a good chance to overcome in the battle against pests.

THE CAMPFIRE

OFTEN at a picnic, after the usual shower, it becomes necessary to build a fire quickly in order to warm up. Where can dry kindling be found? One good thing to remember is that the small dead branches on the lower part of a fir or spruce are practically always dry, can be broken without an axe, and are easily started with a match even if you haven't any wax paper from sandwich wrappings. Small dead trees are the next addition to the fire. Standing timber is always drier than "down" stuff. Dry Aspen Poplar makes a quick and almost smokeless fire. Indians used it when in enemy territory. Pitchy pine, fir or tamarack is good kindling but sends up volumes of dense black smoke. Besides the few hardwoods, larch is probably the best firewood in the Northwest. Fir and pine are more commonly used because they are more abundant.

Build your fire carefully. Especially if you have only one match and are in a hurry. It is helpful to lay it between stones or green logs and then not smother the first small blaze with large pieces of wood.

Be careful with fire. Our forests are one of our greatest resources. Keep your fire away from combustible material. In dry weather an apparently dead fire can "crawl" through a bed of dead needles and blaze into a million dollar fire. Cigarette butts are exceptionally dangerous. Eighty-four percent of forest fires are started by man.

THE PICTURED KEY

A TAXONOMIST'S key consists of a series of clues, such as Sherlock Holmes might use, which by process of elimination bring the searcher to the right name and description of the plant or animal in question. Often these keys are so crowded with eight cylinder words and unfamiliar terms that to any one other than a trained scientist they are more of a hindrance than a help.

In this book we have tried to use simple terms and pictures not only in the key but also in the index to assist the beginner in his sleuthing. Then also the species itself is pictured and the outstanding characteristics graphically shown.

Suppose we key a specimen together. Our tree is not very large, it has awl-shaped leaves in 3's on the twigs, the fruit is a blue berry. Let us start at the beginning of the key at 1a. Leaves absent? No. 1b says Leaves present? Yes, so we go on to 2a. Leaves netted-veined? The illustration shows us this is not it. 2b Leaves parallel-veined, needle-like, awl-like, or scale-like. That seems to be it and we go on to 3a. Palm-like or Yucca-like? No. 3b leads us to 4a and we see that this is not it but at 5a we see what we are looking for. Leaves awl-like or scale-like? That is it and we are directed to 52 which includes the Junipers, Cypresses, and Cedars.

Paging through the book to 52a we read, Fruit cone-like? No, these are the Cypresses and Cedars. 52b Fruit berry-like leads us to the Junipers at 63a. Here it is plainly described and pictured, the COMMON JUNIPER. It so happens that this is the only Juniper in the book with awl-like leaves. The key goes on to the others at 63b because the scale-like leaves are also included in 52b which led us to 63.

Sometimes there are trees that do not seem to fit in with the rest of their relatives, but you will find that the fruit is usually a better indication of where they belong than are the leaves. Because leaf characters are also used in the key we have in some cases cross-keyed certain species so they may be found by more than one key path.

An unusual feature of this book is the additional tabular key to the conifers on page 23. With it you can quickly run down a specimen and then verify your conclusions from the description and picture in the text.

Success to you in your sleuthing. It can be a lot of fun. May your series of clues lead to deductions as marvelous as those of the celebrated Dr. Holmes.

TREE NAMES

 OST people shy away from Latin names for plants and animals, preferring to call them by their common names. We would, too, but the difficulty is that the common names are not the same for a specified tree in all localities. For this reason we will give, in capital letters, the common name used in the United States Department of Agriculture Check List 1953 edition together with the scientific name of each tree. Then there can be no doubt which tree is under discussion.

The scientific name consists of two terms—binomial nomenclature. The first name is always capitalized and refers to the genus. The second is not capitalized; it refers to the species. Both are italicized. If there is a third italicized name it refers to the subspecies. The unitalicized abbreviation after the Latin name is that of the scientist who first officially described and named the species.

Some of the Latin names are exceptionally long and put a severe strain on the jaw. In general, it is good to remember the rule of accenting the second last syllable in scientific names.

The beauty—in case you missed it—of the Latin naming is that it provides one name for a plant throughout the world. The Japanese common name for a tree may mean very little to us, but when we see it referred to as a *Acer japonicum,* we know that it is a Japanese species of Maple.

You may wonder why we write White Fir and Douglas-fir, making it two words in one case and hyphenated in the other. The reason is that the White Fir is a true fir, while the Douglas-fir is not. The rule applies in a number of cases throughout the list of trees. You will also notice that many names ordinarily hyphenated are here spelled as single words according to the revised nomenclature.

TREE HOBBIES, STUDIES, AND PROJECTS

DOUBTLESS there are hundreds of different things that a person who is really interested in trees can find to do in studying them. Any direct contact with them will be of greater value than just reading about them or looking at them. We have here listed a number of hobbies, studies and projects that one might want to investigate. They are given as suggestions and can be worked out according to individual tastes and desires.

1. Leaves of all the trees found in your locality or on your travels may be collected and mounted in a scrap book. They may be fastened with scotch tape or mucilage after they have been pressed between blotters. Information lettered beneath the specimens should contain at least the common and scientific names, and the place where it was found. The leaves should be grouped by families, preferably in the order they are listed in the back of this book. (Fig. 26)

2. Tree blossoms could be mounted in the same way or included with the leaves. In the case of blossoms the date on which they are collected would also be important data.

3. Blue printing or photography can be used in making a collection of leaf silhouettes. They lie flatter than a collection of pressed leaves.

4. Spatter prints can be made by placing the leaf flat on a sheet of paper

Figure 26

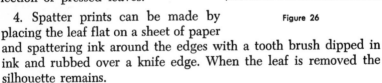

and spattering ink around the edges with a tooth brush dipped in ink and rubbed over a knife edge. When the leaf is removed the silhouette remains.

5. Crayon prints can be made by laying the leaf bottom up on the table and after placing a moderately thin sheet of paper on it rub over the leaf with a crayon. The shading will not only reveal the outline of the leaf but also the venation. Autumn colors can be shown with different colored crayons.

6. Prints can also be made with printer's ink. A roller is used to roll the ink on the surface of the leaf. Then the leaf is laid on the paper, ink down, and a clean piece of newspaper is placed over the leaf. Now pressure is applied over the leaf with the fingers. A new piece of newspaper should be used for every leaf unless you prefer smudges and fingerprints around the leaf print. A little experience will soon teach one how much ink to use and also how to apply the pressure. After the prints are dry they can be bound in booklet form.

Figure 27

7. If leaves are suspended in warm water for a time the softer parts will be eaten out by bacterial action, leaving only the vascular tissue. A collection of all the different types of vein formation can be made in this way. (Fig. 27)

8. Seeds are interesting and could be collected, but would have to be mounted in boxes or under glass. They should be properly labeled and the time of ripening recorded.

9. Twig collections with sectional views of the different types provide interest and useful information.

10. To collect wood from different trees will take a bit more effort, but is certainly worth while. Sections of dry wood should be cut as nearly uniform in size as possible. (Fig. 28) Care should be

Figure 28

taken not to damage ornamental trees in your collecting. One end of the blocks should be cut at right angles, the other end at a 45° angle and a slice planed off the top and bottom. When the flat surfaces are sanded and the whole thing shellacked the grain on three surfaces will show up beautifully and the bark will have an added luster. The flat surface of the bottom will allow the pieces to sit flat and uniformly and not roll.

11. Bark can be collected from mature trees and mounted as were the twigs and wood samples.

12. Galls from the various different trees could be collected and a study made of the causes.

13. The uses of the different trees can be made into a very interesting study. Their different characteristics make them particularly adapted to certain specific uses. A neighbor was cutting some cottonwood logs for a sawmill. They were to be cut into planks that were to be made into vats for seasoning wines. Cottonwood was used because it would not taint the liquor. In discussing it we also found that it was used for shelves for seasoning cheese, and for veneer strawberry boxes. It makes poor firewood, but is excellent to keep a slow fire over night.

14. The folklore of trees and the origin of common names can also become a fascinating hobby.

15. The history and age of trees as revealed by growth rings can be an interesting subject for research. Enos A. Mills' "Story of a Thousand Year Pine" is an illustration of what can be done with a subject such as this.

16. The study of the germination of tree seeds and the growth of various types of seedlings can be fascinating. Especially if one has a movie camera and can take time lapse pictures and compare the growth of different ones in projection later on. (Fig. 29)

Figure 29

17. Grafting can provide much enjoyment. The experience of bridge grafting to save a girdled tree, working over a young tree or grafting several varieties of fruit on a single tree is certainly rewarding. I know of one boy who grafted 12 varieties of fruit on one tree. You may be sure that his friends and visitors never saw the last of it.

18. Planting trees in yards, campuses, orchards or reforestation projects is a real experience to one who loves to see things grow. The raising of trees from cuttings and experimenting with plant hormones on different trees can afford much pleasure and can even develop into a life occupation.

19. Pruning is interesting work. It is a reward in itself to see how long-neglected trees will revive with proper attention. Certain evergreens can be clipped into many different shapes for ornament and curiosity.

20. A good group project is to plant an arboretum, where as many different varieties of trees as possible can be studied at first hand.

21. Label the different trees on the school campus in some permanent way. The common and scientific names should appear on the tag.

$$BC = \frac{DE \times AC}{AE} \text{ or}$$

$$\text{height} = \frac{8 \times 100}{10} = 80$$

Figure 30

22. Map a given area marking the different trees to be found on it.

23. Take a census of the trees in the neighborhood to see which are most abundant and which are most rare. Try to determine why.

24. Measure trees by the method diagrammed and determine the size of the tallest trees in the neighborhood. Also find the ones with the largest diameter. (Fig. 30)

BIG TREES

Along our west coast from San Francisco to Alaska grow some of the tallest trees on the continent. They are the Firs, Douglas-firs, and Redwoods. Further inland, in the mountains east of Fresno, California, grow the Sequoias. One of these, the McKinley Tree, has a base diameter of 30 feet and a height of 291 feet. Another, the General Grant, has a diameter of 40 feet, a height of 267 feet, and contains enough lumber to build 50 six-room houses.

As with humans, however, those largest in girth are not always the tallest. The coast redwoods, though some are wide enough at the base to allow a car to pass through, do not reach the diameter of the Sequoias but grow to 368 feet tall. This seems to be the record for America though a Sequoia in Calaveras Grove is estimated to have been 400 feet high when it was standing according to the American Forestry Association report in *Knowing Your Trees.*

We quoted in the previous edition of this book the record from the Canadian Forestry Association's publication the record of a Douglas-fir that was supposed to have been 25 feet in diameter and 417 feet tall. Since then we have found that this tree was invented by some Canadian lumbermen to put one over their American counterparts at a gathering. The legend has died hard. It was published again just recently in a nature encyclopedia.

Figure 31

The tallest Douglas-fir of which we have record was cut at Ryderwood, Washington, and was 325 feet long, according to the National Geographic Magazine of July 1964. Sitka Spruce have been recorded at 280 feet and Grand Fir at 250-300 feet according to the American Forestry Association.

Other real giants of the tree world are some of the Eucalyptus of Australia. According to John Sidney, an Australian writing in the Natural History Magazine of September 1957, there were two Giant Gums near Thorpedale, Victoria, that were 375 and 331 feet tall. The latter was named after Mark Twain. It was destroyed in a bush fire some time ago and probably the other also. According to the same author, Alfred Russell Wallace, the noted scientist of Darwin's time, wrote of a fallen eucalyptus that was 450 feet long. These giants have all gone, but the tallest Gum still living is 320 feet high. It was discovered in Tasmania in 1956 and it is possible that trees will still be discovered somewhere that are still taller than any we now know.

In this connection, we must not forget still another remarkable tree, the Montezuma Baldcypress, *Taxodium mucronatum*. This species is related to the sequoias and has some of its characteristics of longevity and size. The record tree is located in Santa Maria del Tule, near Oaxaca, Mexico. Its circumference at a height of 4 1/2 feet from the ground is 114 feet, which is 13 feet more than the girth of the largest sequoia. In height the Cypress of Tule is no record breaker, for it is hardly 150 feet tall. Due to some accident in its past history the trunk is greatly divided and branched. Estimates of its age run from 4,000 to 10,000 years, but it is likely that it is not much older than the oldest Redwood, Juniper, or Bristlecone Pine.

Growth rings indicate the oldest sequoias to be between 3,000 and 4,000 years old. They are generally thought to be the oldest living things. It is, however, possible that some of the slow-growing western junipers, small and stunted in comparison, though with girths up to 21 feet, may rival them in age. Growth rings on some of these junipers are as dense as 400 to the inch. By comparison, note that young Douglas-fir or spruce often have as few as four and six rings to the inch. Sitka Spruce for aeroplane wood must have at least eight rings to the inch. A lot of it does not.

Recent borings on the trunks of bristlecone pine trees in the higher levels of the Sierras have shown that they are among the oldest living things if not the oldest with an estimated age of over 4,000 years.

TABULAR KEY FOR THE PINACEAE FAMILY

NAME	Needle length	Needle number	Cone size	Needle color	REMARKS
Coulter Pine	9 "	3	12 "	DBG	Beaked cones
Digger Pine	10 "	3	8 "	GrG	Forked trunks
Knobcone Pine	5 "	3	5½"	LG	Clustered cones
Monterey Pine	5 "	3	5 "	DG	Near Monterey, Calif.
Ponderosa Pine	7 "	3	4½"	YG	Cinnamon bark
Arizona Pine	6 "	3	2 "	GrG	Small cones
Jeffrey Pine	6½"	3	10 "	BG	Large cones
Lodgepole Pine	2 "	2	1½"	BrYG	Slender trunks
Jack Pine	1 "	2	1½"	GrYG	Scrubby
Bishop Pine	4 "	2	3 "	YG	Heavily branched
Singleleaf Pinyon	1½"	1	2 "	GrYG	High altitudes
Parry Pinyon	1½"	4	2 "	BG	Bushy tree
Pinyon	1½"	2	1½"	BG	Mottled nuts
Mexican Pinyon	1½"	3	1½"	BG	Nuts 3-angled
Western White Pine	2½"	5	8 "	BG	Slender cones
Sugar Pine	3 "	5	14 "	BG	Long, slender cones
Torrey Pine	10 "	5	5 "	GrG	Long needles
Foxtail Pine	1 "	5	3½"	BrBG	Slender cones
Bristlecone Pine	1 "	5	3 "	DG	Bristles on cones
Whitebark Pine	2 "	5	2 "	DG	Rounded cones
Limber Pine	2 "	5	6 "	DG	Cones long
Tamarack	1 "	16	¾"	YG	Twigs pliable
Western Larch	1 "	24	1¼"	YG	Twigs brittle
Alpine Larch	¾"	35	1¾"	BG	High altitudes

NAME	Needle length	Cone Color	Cone size	Needle color	REMARKS
Brewer Spruce	1 "	P-G	3¼"	DYG	Drooping branchlets
Sitka Spruce	¾"	LBrn	3 "	BrG	Needles prickly
Englemann Spruce	1 "	LBrn	2½"	DBG	Needles softer
Blue Spruce	1 "	G-P-Brn	3 "	SBG	Silvery blue needles
White Spruce	¾"	G-Brn	2 "	LBG	Cone scales rounded
Black Spruce	½"	P-Brn	1 "	DBG	Abundant cones
Norway Spruce	¾"	LBrn	1 "	DG	Long cones
Western Hemlock	½"	P-RBrn	1 "	BrG	YG branch tips
Mountain Hemlock	½"	P-YG	1½"	GrBG	High altitudes
Douglas-fir	1 "	R-Brn	2½"	BrG	3-pointed bracts
Bigcone Douglas-fir	1 "	DBrn	4½"	GrG	Large cones
Subalpine Fir	1½"	G-P	3 "	BG	High altitudes
Noble Fir	1 "	R-YG	5 "	BG	Cone bracts showing
Pacific Silver Fir	1¼"	P-DP	4½"	DG	Smooth bark
White Fir	2 "	G-P	4 "	GW	Rough bark
Grand Fir	2 "	YG	3 "	YG	YG cones
California Red Fir	1 "	G-R-P	5½"	BG	Large cones

B—blue, Br—bright, Brn—brown, D—dark, G—green, Gr—gray, L—light, P—purple, R—red, S—silver, W—white, Y—yellow.

PICTURED KEY FOR IDENTIFYING WESTERN TREES
THE EVERGREENS

1a Leaves absent, fleshy, succulent, trunks and branches spiny. The CACTI ....page 126

1b Leaves present 2

2a Leaves netted-veined. Fig. 32. The BROADLEAFS ......page 61

Figure 32

2b Leaves parallel-veined, needle-like, awl-like or scale-like 3

3a Leaves palm-like or yucca-like ....page 57

3b Leaves not as above 4

4a Leaves fan-like, veins radial, fruit a nut. Fig. 33. GINKGO, ...*Ginkgo biloba* L.

This native of China grows up to 120′ tall and has deciduous, light gray, outer bark. The fan-shaped leaves mark it as being different from any tree one is likely to see except among fossils. Flowers are of two kinds and the yellow-orange apricot-like fruit contains a single white-shelled nut. These nuts are eaten at wedding feasts in China.

Figure 33

4b Not as above 5

5a Leaves awl-like or scale-like. Fig. 34. JUNIPERS, CYPRESSES, and CEDARS 52

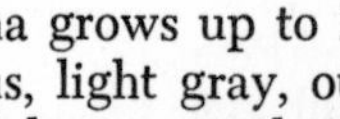

Figure 34

5b Leaves needle-like. Fig. 35. ....…...................6

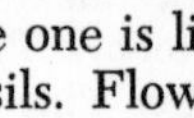

Figure 35

6a Needles in bundles. Fig. 36. PINES and LARCHES 7

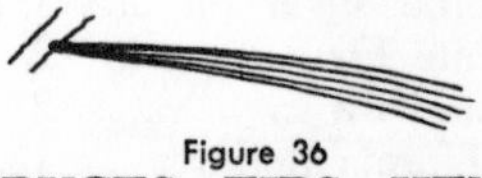

Figure 36

6b Needles growing singly on twigs. SPRUCES, FIRS, HEM-LOCKS and YEWS 30

7a Needles in bundles of 5 or less. PINES 8

7b Needles deciduous, in bundles of 12-30. LARCHES 28

A tree up to 60′ tall, short-trunked, heavy-limbed. The bark is dark brown, roughly furrowed. Needles dark blue-green, dense, 6″-12″ long, in bundles of 3. Male flowers are yellow, female are dark reddish with a white bloom. The golden brown cones are 9″-14″ long, and weigh 4-5 pounds. Scales have strong recurved beaks. It is used for cheap lumber, fuel and charcoal.

Figure 37

13b Cones 6″-10″ long, beaks not exceptionally large, trunks often forking. Fig. 38. ....DIGGER PINE, *Pinus sabiniana* Dougl.

A tree growing up to 80′ tall, bushy, open top, trunk usually forking into two or more main branches. The bark is dull brown, scaly, deeply fissured, and thick. Needles are gray-green, 7″-13″ long, in bundles of 3. They drop after 3-4 years, leaving branches bare. Female flowers are reddish. The mature cones are reddish brown, asymmetrical, long-stalked, with pitchy scale tips armed with strong recurved beaks. It is used for fuel and cheap lumber and grows on dry gravelly hillsides.

Figure 38

14a Cones slender, asymmetrical, persist in dense clusters. Fig. 39.
.... KNOBCONE PINE, *Pinus attenuata* Lemm.

This tree grows up to 40′ tall with branches that are upcurved and heavily laden near the trunk with persistent cones. The bark is dull brown, in thin, loose scales that form shallow ridges. The needles are light green, rigid, 3″-7″ long, in bundles of 3. The male flowers are found in clusters on the branch tips, the female are often in pairs. The hard, lopsided cones often have a few beaks on the convex side. They persist in heavy clusters on the trunk and branches until the death of the tree and do not open till after a fire. It is valuable as a ground cover to shelter more valuable trees after a forest fire.

Figure 39

14b Cones more egg-shaped, not persisting 15

15a Cones heavier than 14a, grows in a restricted area along the coast. Fig. 40. ......MONTEREY PINE, *Pinus radiata* D. Don

This tree is up to 100′ tall with a dense, rounded top and open trunk. The bark is nearly black, hard, roughly fissured and thick. The dark green needles are 3 1/2″-6″ long, usually 3 in a bundle, sometimes 2. Male flowers are catkin-like at the branch ends, female are purplish. The dark, russet-brown cones are 3″-7″ long, lopsided, persist 6-10 years and have black seeds. These pines are pleasing for ornamental use or for windbreaks.

Figure 40

15b Inland forest trees, cones more symmetrical 16

16a Cones 3″-6″ long, needles yellow-green. Fig. 41. ....
............................PONDEROSA PINE, *Pinus ponderosa* Laws.

Usually known as the WESTERN YELLOW PINE, this tree grows up to 230′ tall, the crown is flat-topped or rounded and the branches are heavy and horizontal, the lower trunk is usually clear. The bark is a bright, cinnamon red on older trees, to black on younger ones. It is broken into large plates which break up into smaller irregularly-lobed sections. The needles are yellow-green, 4″-11″ long, in bundles of 3, and form tufts at the ends of branches. The male flowers form yellow clusters at the branch ends, the female are dark red. The cones are green and erect till the 2nd year then turn brown, droop and open. This is a valuable tree for building lumber, box wood and firewood. Log-

Figure 41

gers often refer to the trees with a proportionately large and pitchy heartwood as BULL PINE, but needle and cone character-istics are identical with the others.

—ARIZONA PINE, *P. p. arizonica,* Shaw. is the variety found in Arizona, Chihuahua and Sonora, needles are more gray-green than in the species and cones are smaller.

—ROCKY MOUNTAIN PINE, *P. p. scopulorum* Englem. Found from Texas to Montana on the eastern slope of the Rockies.

16b Cones 5″-15″ long, needles blue-green. Fig. 42. ....
...........................JEFFREY PINE, *Pinus jeffreyi* **Grev. & Balf.**

This tree grows up to 150′ tall, is simi-lar to the Ponderosa, but smaller and stouter. The bark characteristics are the same, but the smaller twigs are more purple. The needles are bluish-green, 4″-9″ long, in bundles of 3. Male flow-ers are yellow-green, the female are purplish. The cones are purple to brown, 5″-15″ long and denser than the Pon-derosa. The prickles turn in on the open cone. Lumber is used for building, box-wood and fuel.

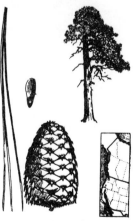

Figure 42

17a Cones tapered, in pairs, smooth, incurved. Fig. 43. ....
....JACK PINE, *Pinus banksiana* Lamb.

This is a scrubby tree of the northern plains. It grows up to 70′ tall, has an open, round top and a straight trunk. The bark is dark, reddish brown, thin and close-scaled. The needles are grayish yellow-green, in bundles of 2 and clustered around the new growth, they are 3/4″-1 1/2″ long. The male catkins are in short, yellow clusters. The cones are dark purple turning to grayish brown, in hard, incurved pairs persisting for 25-30 years. It is chiefly useful for fuel, pulp, rough timber, packing cases, posts and mine timbers. It is particularly useful in mines because it creaks a warning before giving way. Like the western congener, the Lodgepole, it makes a good ground cover after fires or logging operations.

Figure 43

17b Cones in pairs, prickly 18

18a Trees tall and slender, in dense stands, needles 1 1/2″-3″ long. Fig. 44. ....
............LODGEPOLE PINE, *Pinus contorta latifolia* Engelm.

The Lodgepole Pine grows in thick stands, is tall and straight and is branched only on the upper quarter. It grows up to 100′ tall and has bark that is dark brown to orange, scaly and thin. The needles are bright yellow-green, in bundles of 2, 1″-3″ long. The male catkins are reddish, the cones are purple, turning to light yellow-brown when mature. They are prickly and incurved. Some drop annually, others remain on the tree and do not open until after a forest fire. Indians used the slender poles for their teepees and the sap for liquor. They are now used for lumber, fuel, mine props, ties, fence posts, corral poles, and cabin logs. To foresters their main use is as a cover crop after a forest fire to help other trees get started.

Figure 44

—SHORE PINE *P. contorta* Dougl. is the name given to the coast type. This tree grows singly, is stunted and usually greatly twisted.

18b Needles 3″-5″ long, cones small and beaked. Fig. 45. ....
....**BISHOP PINE,** *Pinus muricata* **D. Don**

A small scrubby tree, up to 60′ tall, with a dense, rounded top, branched right to the ground. The bark is dark, purplish brown, scaly and deeply furrowed. The yellow-green needles in bundles of 2 are 3″-5″ long, in dense clusters at the end of the branches. Both male and female flowers are clustered at branch ends. The mature cones are unsymmetric, 2″-3 1/2″ long, have spurred scales and persist indefinitely. Seeds are large and black. The trees are used for firewood, but are too stunted for commercial use.

Figure 45

19a Needles usually single, sometimes 2. Fig. 46. ....
......**SINGLELEAF PINYON,** *Pinus monophylla* **Torr. & Frem.**

A low, spreading tree, up to 50′ tall, the trunk usually divides into several large branches near the base. The bark is dull gray to brown, irregularly fissured, having thin scales. Leaves are pale yellow-green, stiff, prickly, curved inward, 1 1/2″ long, usually single. The male flowers are in dark red spikes; the female, in purplish clusters that mature into dark-brown, shiny cones, 1 1/2″-2″ long, oblong. The nuts are large and short-winged. This tree finds some use as fuel and fence posts, but its main value is in the nuts which are prized as food.

Figure 46

19b Needles more than 1 to a bundle **20**

20a Needles 4 to a bundle. Fig. 47. ....……...................
..................................**PARRY PINYON,** *Pinus quadrifolia* **Parl.**

This tree is up to 40′ tall, bushy, having a dense crown and a short trunk. The bark is reddish brown and the scales, plate-like. The pale bluish-green leaves are stiff, curved, up to 1 1/2″ long and usually in bundles of 4. The brown cones are stubby, 1 1/4″-2 1/4″ long, fall apart easily and the nuts drop out leaving the narrow wing on the scale. They are highly prized for food by both Indians and white people.

Figure 47

20b Needles 2-3 in a bundle ....…....................**21**

21a Needles in bundles of 2. Fig. 48. ....
..............................…........................ **PINYON,** *Pinus edulis* **Engelm.**

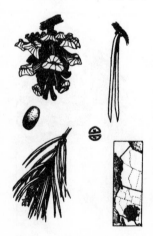

This pinyon grows up to 50′ tall with a rounded crown and low horizontal branches. The bark is reddish brown and has irregular zig-zag furrows. The bright blue-green needles are sharp-pointed, curved, 1″-1 3/4″ long, and usually in bundles of 2. The male flowers are dark red, elongate and in clusters. The female cones are purplish, abundant all over the tree at the branch ends. They mature into yellowish brown, egg-shaped cones, 1″-2″ long. The nuts are reddish brown and mottled. They are roasted and eaten as food.

Figure 48

21b Needles mostly 2 in a bundle, sometimes 3, seeds slightly 3-angled. Fig. 49. ....
.............................MEXICAN PINYON, *Pinus cembroides* Zucc.

The tree is bush-like, up to 30' tall, trunk short, branches heavy and wide-spreading. The bark is reddish brown and the thick scales are arranged in wide ridges. The short, pale, bluish-green needles are usually in bundles of 3, but also in 2's and 4's. The male flowers grow in catkin-like clusters, the female cones are abundant on the branch tips. The cones are brownish and stubby and the nuts are large and wingless. They are widely eaten for food in the area where the tree is found.

Figure 49

22a Cones long, 6"-20", slender when closed 23

22b Cones shorter 24

23a Cones 6"-10" long. Fig. 50. ....
.................WESTERN WHITE PINE, *Pinus monticola* Dougl.

A straight, clear-trunked tree, up to 200' tall, with a narrow, pyramidal crown and short, drooping branches. The bark is a deep violet-gray to reddish, finely fissured and has tight scales. The pale, blue-green needles are 1"-4" long and in bundles of 5. The male flowers are in clusters of 6-7 catkins, the female cones are pale purplish, standing erect on the branch tips near the top of the tree. The mature yellow-brown cones are slender, 6"-10" long and pendulous. The lumber is excellent for door and window cases, shelving, match sticks and moulding. It is easily worked and ideally suited to pattern making.

Figure 50

23b Cones 8"-20" long. Fig. 51. ....
..............................SUGAR PINE, *Pinus lambertiana* Dougl.

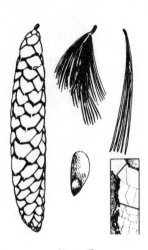

Figure 51

A straight, clear-trunked tree, up to 240' tall, with a spire-like to flat-topped crown and a dense foliage on the heavy, horizontal branches. The bark is reddish brown to dark gray, broken by irregular fissures. A sweet, white resin oozes out of cuts. The deep, blue-green needles are 2 1/2"-4" long, in bundles of 5. The male flowers are long-stalked, pale yellow, in clusters. The female are light green to pale violet, erect cones. When mature they turn dark purple to brown, slender cones, 8"-20" are long and pendulous. The wood is excellent for building lumber, interior finish, pattern and model work. The Indians were fond of the sweet sap and traveled long distances to find it.

24a Stunted coast trees, north of San Diego, needles 8"-12" long. Fig. 52. ....TORREY PINE, *Pinus torreyana* Parry

Figure 52

A crooked tree, of irregular shape, bent by the sea winds, up to 60' tall. The bark is pale, reddish brown, irregularly broken into spongy, flat, wide scales. The dark, gray-green needles in bundles of 5 are 8"-12" long and tend to cluster on branch tips. The male flowers are yellow and grow in dense heads. The female are purplish cones that turn from russet to chocolate brown when mature. They are plump, 4"-6" long and grow on long stalks. The seeds are large, nearly surrounded by a thin, brown wing and are edible raw or roasted. The tree, being rare and restricted to a few miles of coastline just north of San Diego, California, is protected and of no commercial importance.

24b Trees not restricted to the coastline, needles shorter 25

25a Cones distinctly prickly 26

25b Cones not prickly 27

26a Cones 2 1/2"-5" long, prickles minute, branches bushy. Fig.
    53. ....FOXTAIL PINE, *Pinus balfouriana* Grev. & Balf.

A heavy-trunked tree, up to 75' tall, with short, drooping branches. The thin, angular plates of the reddish brown bark form shallow fissures. Bright, blue-green needles, 3/4"-1 1/2" long, in bundles of 5, grow close along the branch except at the end where they flare out into a foxtail. This characteristic gives the tree its name. The slender cones, 2 1/2"-5" long, are russet brown and have scales with thickened ends and small prickles. The tree is of no commercial use since it is found only in high altitudes and is rare.

Figure 53

26b Cones 2 1/2"-3 1/2" long, prickles prominent, 1/4" long. Fig.
    54. ....BRISTLECONE PINE, *Pinus aristata* Engelm.

This tree of the high altitudes is usually stunted and bushy, but will grow up to 45' tall. The branches are short and stout and the trunk is thick. The dull, reddish brown, scaly bark is broken into shallow furrows. The needles are deep green, 1/2"-1 1/2" long, 5 to a bundle, and clasp the branches densely like the Foxtail Pine. Male flowers form dark, red-orange spikes, the female are dark purple. They change to deep chocolate brown cones, 2 1/2"-3 1/2" long, and are pendant on the branch tips. The scales have thin bristles on them that are about 1/4" long. There is no commercial value attached to this tree since it is rather rare and found only in the high altitudes.

Figure 54

27a Bark white, thin, and scaly. Fig. 55. ....
...........................WHITEBARK PINE, *Pinus albicaulis* **Engelm.**

This is another tree of the high altitudes, usually between 5000' and the
timberline. It is dwarfed, has long, low
branches, but gets to be 50' tall at best.
The bark is silvery white and thin. On
young trees it is pinkish. The dark green
needles are 1"-2 1/2" long, in bundles
of 5, and grow only at the branch tips.
The male flowers form showy scarlet
catkins. The cones are purple, changing
at maturity to brown. They are ball-
shaped, 1"-3" long, and clustered at
branch ends. Mature cones are not common. Because of its inaccessibility and
stunted nature it has little commercial
value.

Figure 55

27b Bark brown, rough and thick, twigs long and flexible. Fig. 56.
....LIMBER PINE, *Pinus flexilis* **James**

A tree, up to 80' tall, with a wide,
round-topped head. The young branches
are so limber that they can be tied into
knots without breaking. The bark is dark
brown, deeply furrowed and broken into
plates. The dark green needles are
1 1/2"-3" long, in bundles of 5, and
grow in close-curving masses at the
branch ends. The male flowers grow in
reddish spikes, the female in red-violet
clusters near the top of the tree. Mature
cones are greenish to buff colored,
4"-10" long. The cone scales are thickened, but without barbs. The seeds are
large and hard-shelled. It is used for
fuel and building timber.

Figure 56

—*P. f. reflexa* Engelm. is a variety listed because of its noticeably
recurved branch tips.

28a Cones small with short bracts. Fig. 57. ....
....TAMARACK, *Larix laricina* K. Koch

An eastern tree, the tamarack does not reach much more than 60' in height in the western areas where it grows. It is straight and symmetrical, and has a spire-like crown. The bark is reddish brown, scaly and only about 1/2" thick. The yellow-green needles are triangular in cross-section, pointed, 3/4"-1 1/4" long, in bundles of 12-20 and deciduous. The male flowers are small, yellow and in clusters, the cones are rosy and round. They mature into chestnut-brown cones with thin scales and short bracts. They are 1/2"-3/4" long and mature annually. The wood of this tree is used for ties, posts, poles and building lumber.

Figure 57

28b Cones larger with protruding bracts 29

29a Needles in bundles of 15-30, trees spire-like. Fig. 58. ....
...........................WESTERN LARCH, *Larix occidentalis* Nutt.

A straight-trunked, forest tree, up to 200' tall, with a spire-like crown and small branches. The bark is cinnamon red, flaky and deeply furrowed at the base. Surface knots or burls are common. It resembles *Pinus ponderosa* in appearance. The pale yellow-green needles are 1"-1 1/4" long, in bundles of 15-30 and turn bright yellow in fall before dropping. The male flowers are yellow-green, 1/4" in diameter. Bright red female flowers grow on the same twigs and mature into light brown cones, 1"-1 1/2" long, with thin scales and prominently protruding bracts. Important commercially for ties, posts, siding, firewood, poles, piles, flooring, interior finish, boats and window sash.

Figure 58

29b Needles in bundles of 30-40, grows in high altitudes. Fig. 59.
.....................................SUBALPINE LARCH, *Larix lyalli* Parl.

This high altitude tree is stunted and crooked, up to 40' tall, new shoots on the branches are covered with fine white wool. The bark is reddish brown to purple, and is scaled rather than furrowed. The 4-angled, light bluish-green needles are 1/2"-1" long, in bundles of 30-40 and turn lemon yellow before dropping in fall. Male flowers are greenish; female, reddish in color. The mature cones are purple, 1 1/2"-2" long and bristly with exserted bracts. The tree is of no commercial value because it is rare and found only near the timberline.

Figure 59

30a Needles usually in flat sprays. HEMLOCKS, YEWS, TORREYAS, and REDWOOD 47

30b Needles not in flat sprays. SPRUCES, FIRS, and DOUGLAS-FIRS 31

31a Cones pendant, entire cones deciduous. SPRUCES and DOUGLAS-FIRS 32

31b Cones erect, scales deciduous, needles sessile. FIRS 42

Figure 60

32a Cones with 3-pointed bracts protruding, bark heavy. DOUGLAS-FIRS 41

Figure 61

32b Cones other than above 33

33a Needles flattened, grooved, and stalked. HEMLOCKS 40

Figure 62

33b Needles usually 4-angled, leaf base persistent. SPRUCES 34

Figure 63

34a Needles angled but flattened 35

34b Needles more square in cross-section 36

35a Cones long and slender, scales broad, branchlets drooping. Fig. 64. ....BREWER SPRUCE, *Picea breweriana* Wats.

Also called Weeping Spruce, this tree is up to 70′ tall, has a pointed crown, upturned branches with pendant branchlets. The dark, reddish brown bark has thin, firm scales. The needles are flattened, deep yellow-green, 3/4″-1 1/4″ long, and dense on the twig. The male flowers are drooping, the female, erect and larger. The cones mature in one season, are purple to green, 3″-3 1/4″ long, slender and pendulous. This tree is rare and inaccessible because of its high mountain habitat.

Figure 64

35b Cones oblong, scales papery, elliptic and concave, trunk buttressed. Fig. 65. ....SITKA SPRUCE, *Picea sitchensis* Carr.

A stately tree, up to 200′ tall, with a narrow crown, horizontal branches and a buttressed trunk. The reddish brown bark has small loose scales. The flattened needles are 4-angled, sharp-pointed, bright green, 1/2″-1″ long, and dense all around the twig. The crimson male flowers are on the drooping side branches, the female are higher up. The buff-colored, papery-scaled cones are 2″-4″ long. The light, straight-grained wood is used for construction of planes, ladders, boats, venetian blinds, and sounding boards for pianos.

Figure 65

36a Bark reddish brown, thin and scaly 37

36b Bark ashy gray to brown 38

37a Cones 1"-3" long, scale irregularly notched. Fig. 66. ....
.................ENGELMANN SPRUCE, *Picea engelmannii* **Parry**

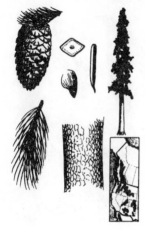

Figure 66

A heavy-trunked tree, up to 125' tall, with a pyramidal crown and drooping branches. The bark is reddish brown and thin with small, loose scales. The dark blue-green needles are 4-angled, 1" long, spiral on the twig and softer to touch than on the Sitka Spruce. The male flowers are dark purple, the female, bright red. The cones are light brown, 1"-3" long, and distinguished from the Sitka Spruce in that the lower edges of the scales are ruffled. The wood is used for pulp, box wood and building timber. It is white, soft and weak.

37b Cones 4"-7" long, abundant. Fig. 67. ....
......................................NORWAY SPRUCE, *Picea excelsa* **Link**

Figure 67

A symmetrical tree, up to 150' tall, with drooping branches, reddish brown, scaly bark that is thin. The needles are shiny, dark green, 4-sided, 3/4" long and surround the twig. It can usually be distinguished from other spruces by the long cones, 4"-7" long that are plentiful in the upper branches. They are erect till fertilized, then drooping. This European tree is much used in shelter belts and windbreaks. Where grown in commercial stands in its native habitat it is used for construction lumber and pulp.

38a Needles silvery blue-green, cones 3"-4" long. Fig. 68..............
....................................BLUE SPRUCE, *Picea pungens* **Engelm.**

A regularly tapered tree up to 120′
tall, with horizontal branches. The bark
is ashy brown, thin. The scales form
rounded ridges. The needles are silvery
green to blue, 1/2"-1 1/4" long, 4-an-
gled and curved. Male flowers are orange; the female, green to purple. The
oblong cones are pale brown, 2 1/2"-4"
long and found in the upper branches.
This tree is used for corral posts and
fuel, but mainly as an ornamental tree.
–KOSTER BLUE SPRUCE, *P. pungens*
kosteriana Mast. is the most popular
variety of blue spruce and is much
planted for its silvery blue-green foliage.

Figure 68

38b Cone scales rounded **39**

39a Needles light blue-green, cones 1 1/2"-2 1/2" long, scales
thin. Fig. 69. ....WHITE SPRUCE, *Picea glauca* **Voss**

A pyramidal tree, up to 100′ tall, with
branches that droop and recurve. It has
bark that is pale, ashy brown, scaly and
thin. The light blue-green needles are
sharp-pointed, 4-angled, dense, and give
off a skunk-like odor when crushed. The
male flowers are orange, the female, are
reddish green. The green cones turn
light brown when mature, they are oval,
1 1/2"-2 1/2" long, pendant and have
scales that are soft and thin. The tree
is used for pulp, building lumber, windbreaks and shade.
–WESTERN WHITE SPRUCE, *P. g.*
albertiana Sarg. Has shorter, broader
cones than the species. It is found in
the southern part of the indicated range.
Variety *porsildii* found in Northwest
British Columbia has smooth bark.

Figure 69

39b Needles deep blue-green, cones 1/2″-1 1/2″ long, scales have uneven, hairy edges. Fig. 70. ....
...................................BLACK SPRUCE, *Picea mariana* **B.S.P.**

A narrow-crowned tree, up to 50′ tall, with short branches and a straight, slender trunk. The thin, scaly bark is ashy brown to gray. The deep blue-green needles are 4-angled, 1/2″-3/4″ long, blunt-tipped. Male flowers have reddish anthers, female are purplish in color. The grayish brown cones, 1/2″-1 1/2″ long, have rounded scales with uneven, hairy edges. They remain on the tree for 30-40 years and hang in dense clusters. There is little commercial use for the wood in the west.

Figure 70

40a Cones small, branches in flat sprays. Fig. 71. ....
...................WESTERN HEMLOCK, *Tsuga heterophylla* **Sarg.**

A graceful tree, up to 250′ tall, pyramidal crown, branches drooping, trunk straight, base swollen. Its bark is reddish brown to gray, broken into shallow, narrow furrows. The fresh, green needles are whitish below, 1/4″-1″ long, flattened and in flat sprays that are bright yellow-green at the tips. The yellow male flowers are single at the branch ends. The female are purple, small and scaly, also at the branch ends. Mature cones are reddish brown, 3/4″-1 1/4″ long and plentiful. The upper surface is covered with fine down. The lumber is used for pulp and building. The knots are hard enough to turn the blade of an axe, but the lumber is superior to that of the eastern species.

Figure 71

40b Cones larger, sprays not flattened, grows in high altitudes.
Fig. 72. ....MOUNTAIN HEMLOCK, *Tsuga mertensiana* **Carr.**

A tree with a pyramidal, but irregular crown, up to 150′ tall, with branches thick and rigid. The dark, reddish brown bark is thin and firm and the ridges are narrow. The needles are blue-gray to pale green 1/2″-3/4″ long, blunt, plump looking, and grow all around the branch. The red-violet male flowers grow on slender drooping stems; the female, purple to yellow-green cones are erect. Mature cones are the same color, but pendant in clusters near the branch ends. This tree is usually stunted and inaccessible for commercial use.

Figure 72

41a Cones small, needles bright green. Fig. 73. ....
...........................DOUGLAS-FIR, *Pseudotsuga menziesii* **Franco**

A clear, straight-trunked tree, up to and over 300′ tall, with a spire-like crown. The upper branches point up, the lower ones droop and recurve. The gray to reddish brown bark is thick and deeply furrowed, but soft. On young trees resin blisters are common. The fresh, bright green needles, 3/4″-1 1/4″ long, are flattened, have 2 white stripes below and form spirals on the twig. Male flowers are bright red, female are green and have prominent bracts. Mature cones are reddish brown, 1 1/2″-4 1/2″ long and pendant. Three-pointed bracts extend beyond the cone scale. This tree is very common in the west and is one of the most important lumber trees. It is used for plywood, bridge and building lumber and many other things.

Figure 73

—BLUE DOUGLAS-FIR *P. m. glauca* Franco has leaves that are more bluish-green.

41b Cones twice as large, needles dusty gray-green. Fig. 74. ....
....BIGCONE DOUGLAS-FIR, *Pseudotsuga macrocarpa* **Mayr**

A more irregular trunk, up to 60′ tall, with drooping branches. The reddish brown to black bark is thick, blisters present. The needles are gray-green, 3/4″-1 1/4″ long and pointed. The flowers are similar to *menziesii* but the dark rich brown cones are twice as large, 3 3/4″-6″ long, and have shorter bracts. It is used for firewood. It was formerly called Bigcone-Spruce.

Figure 74

42a Resinous cones, usually in clusters, grows in high altitudes.
Fig. 75. ....SUBALPINE FIR, *Abies lasiocarpa* **Nutt.**

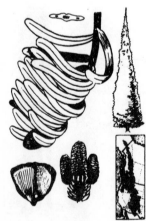

A spire-like tree, up to 90′ tall, lower branches long and drooping. The thin, hard bark is ashy gray to white. The deep blue-green leaves, 1″-1 3/4″ long, are flattened, up-curved and crowded on the twigs. The male flowers are dark blue, the female cones are in erect clusters on the upper branches. When mature they turn a deeper violet and are covered with gum.
—CORKBARK FIR, *A. l. arizonica* Lemm. is shown in stipple on the map.

Figure 75

42b Not as above **43**

43a Cone bracts exserted. Fig. 76. ....
....**NOBLE FIR,** *Abies procera* **Rehd.**

A straight-trunked tree, up to 200' tall, with a round to conical crown. The grayish brown bark is hard and broken into narrow ridges. The upcurved needles are dark blue-green, grooved above, 3/4"-1 1/2" long, and dense. The single male flowers are purple; female are red to yellow-green. The mature cones are clustered at the tree tops, purple to greenish, 4"-6" long, erect with protruding bracts. The wood is used for building lumber and crating.

—BRISTLECONE FIR, *A. bracteata* D. Don. This rare species has cones with long bristlelike bracts showing. Its range is shown by the arrow.

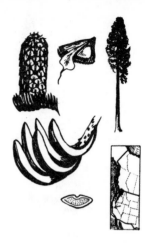

Figure 76

43b Cone bracts not exserted ....**44 also 49**

44a Bark grayish, needles flattened **45**

44b Bark reddish brown **46**

45a Bark smooth, pale gray, needles notched. Fig. 77. ....
...................................**PACIFIC SILVER FIR,** *Abies amabilis* **Frob.**

A tree with a narrow spire-like crown, up to 200' tall, branches drooping gracefully. The bark is ashy gray to white, smooth or finely grooved, resin blisters common. The flattened needles are dark rich green above, silvery white below. They are notched on the lower branches and pointed on the upper, and form 4 ranks on the twig. The male flowers are red, the female, purplish. Mature cones are dark purple, 3 1/2"-6" long, in erect clusters on the upper branches. The wood is used for construction lumber.

Figure 77

45b Bark rough and horny, cones often pitchy. Fig. 78. ....
....WHITE FIR, *Abies concolor* Lindl.

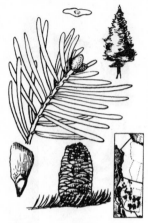

A densely branched tree, up to 200' tall, with a conical crown. The bark is ashy gray, deeply furrowed, rough and hard. On younger branches there are plenty of resin blisters. The flattened leaves are white on both sides and form spirals on the twig. The male flowers are long and scaly and hang from the under side of the branches. The female are short, rounded and erect. The ashy green to purple cones, 3"-5", stand erect and single. The wood is white and is used for building purposes. It is planted as an ornamental tree.

Figure 78

46a Needles flat, notched, cones bright yellow-green. Fig. 79. ......
....GRAND FIR, *Abies grandis* Lindl.

A straight-trunked tree, up to 250' tall, with a narrow crown and branches that droop and recurve. The bark is light brown to white, and forms hard narrow ridges. Resin blisters are common on young trees. The flat, dark yellow-green needles are notched, 1"-2 1/2" long, shiny above, silvery white below, and form sprays that are somewhat flattened. The male flowers are pale yellow, singly attached on the under side of the lower branches. The female cones are yellow-green, scaly and erect on the upper branches. At maturity they are still bright yellow-green 2"-4" long and erect. The wood is used for pulp, boxwood and rough construction.

Figure 79

46b Needles 4-angled, cones large, dark purple. Fig. 80. ....
...................CALIFORNIA RED FIR, *Abies magnifica* **Murr.**

A straight-trunked tree up to 175′ tall with a narrow, cone-shaped crown and drooping branches. The bark is dark brown to black, hard and thick with zigzagged furrows. The dark blue-green needles are 4-angled upcurved and 3/4″-1 1/4″ long. The dark, reddish brown male flowers hang below the lower branches, the green to red female flowers are erect on the upper branches. Mature cones are dark purple, 5″-6″ long, single and erect. The wood has a reddish tint and is used for rough construction.

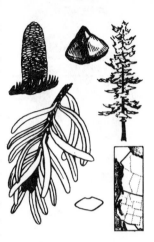

—SHASTA RED FIR *A. m. shastensis* Lemm. is a variety identical with *magnifica* except that the cones have protruding bracts.

Figure 80

47a Fruit cone-like or solid. REDWOODS, HEMLOCKS, and TORREYAS 48

47b Fruit berry-like, seed protruding from the flesh. Fig. 81. ....
......................................PACIFIC YEW, *Taxus brevifolia* **Nutt.**

An unsymmetrical tree that grows up to 40′ tall, has a straight but branched and fluted trunk and drooping branches. The bark is rosy red to purplish in thin papery scales. The flat, pointed, shiny, dark yellow-green needles are 1″ long and form flat sprays. The male flowers are small and yellow, in axillary heads, on trees separate from the female which are greenish and bud-like. The ripened fruit is a pea-sized, coral red berry that is flattened at the calyx showing the one seed. The tree is useful for bow wood, paddles and turning.

—ENGLISH YEW, *Taxus baccata* L. A flat-sprayed European tree, many varieties of which are used in ornamental planting.

Figure 81

48a Fruit woody, nutmeg-like. Fig. 82. ....
..............CALIFORNIA TORREYA, *Torreya californica* **Torr.**

A pyramidal tree that grows up to 70′ tall, has an irregular, convoluted trunk, slender and slightly drooping branches. The bark is pale yellowish brown, soft and finely seamed with long, loose scales. The flat, pointed, shiny, yellow-green needles are 2 1/2″ long, in flat sprays. Male flowers are in small axillary clusters of 6-8 whorls, with 4 stamens each. The female grow singly on branch tips. The green to purple, woody seed is nutmeg-like, 1 1/2″ long. This rare tree grows in the cool canyons of the California coast.

Figure 82

48b Fruit cone-like. REDWOODS and HEMLOCKS 50

49a Leaves overlapping, large pointed scales. Fig. 83. ....
.... MONKEY PUZZLE, *Araucaria araucana* **Koch**

A pyramidal tree, up to 100′ tall, with pale gray bark that shows the regular pattern of leaf scars. The foliage of densely overlapping, sharp-pointed leaf scales is distinctive. Thick milky sap oozes out of cuts. Cones are 5″-8″ long, pineapple-like. This native of Chile is widely grown from Vancouver to San Diego on the coast.

—BUNYA-BUNYA, *A. bidwillii* Hook. This is a tree up to 80′ tall. It has dark green, shining awl-like leaves 1″-3″ long by 1/2″ wide cones 7″-10″ long. It is a native of Australia and is planted in parks in California.

Figure 83

49b Leaves needle-like, cone scales deciduous. Fig. 84. ....
........................NORFOLK ISLAND-PINE, *Araucaria excelsa* R. Br.

A tree up to 70' tall with needles 1/4"-1/2" long, densely covering the twigs. Cones 4"-6" long have scales that drop off liberating the seeds as they mature. There is I seed under each scale. The inverted cone shape of this tree is caused by the whorled branches increasing in size toward the top. The unusual shape makes it a popular tree for garden planting. These trees are native of the Australian region and were first discovered by Captain Cook on his second long voyage. The genus name comes from the Araucanian Indians of Chili, South America. Several relatives, including the Monkey Puzzle Tree, are found in South America.

Figure 84

50a Bark stringy, in long ridges, restricted to California coast. Fig. 85. ....REDWOOD, *Sequoia sempervirens* Endl.

A magnificent forest tree, up to 360' tall and 25' thick. The trunk is straight, buttressed at the base; the branches are short and drooping. The cinnamon-brown, fibrous bark is up to 12" thick and is fire resistant. The dark green needles are flat, sharp-pointed, stiff, and vary from awl-like to 1" in length. They are whitish below. Male flowers are small, greenish yellow; female flowers are egg-shaped, terminal, maturing into purplish brown cones, 1" long with 4 seeds under each scale. The wood is dark, straight-grained, easily worked and is extremely useful for bridge timbers, ties, tanks, flumes, grape stakes, and building.

Figure 85

50b Not as above 51

51a Cones with thin papery scales. HEMLOCKS 40

51b Leaves scale-like, not in flat sprays. Fig. 86. ....
....GIANT SEQUOIA, *Sequoia gigantea* **Decne.**

An inland tree, up to 330' tall, trunk straight, clear, branches heavy. Red-brown bark is spongy, very thick, appears fluted. Overlapping leaf scales are dark green, in clustered sprays. Male and female flowers are minute, on branch tips. The yellow-brown, egg-shaped cones are 2"-3" long. Under each cone scale are 5-7 seeds. The tree is rare—a tourist attraction.

—MONTEZUMA BALDCYPRESS, *Taxodium mucronatum* **Ten.** an enormous tree of central Mexico, related to the sequoias, sometimes planted in parks.

Figure 86

52a Fruit cone-like. CEDARS and CYPRESSES 53

52b Fruit berry-like. JUNIPERS 63

53a Large forest trees 54

53b Ornamental or stunted coast or desert trees 57

54a Cones with 2 scales, seeds ash-like. Fig. 87. ....
........CALIFORNIA INCENSE-CEDAR, *Libocedrus decurrens* **Torr.**

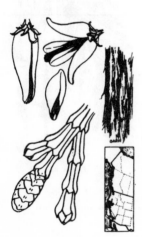

This tree grows up to 150' tall and has a widely buttressed trunk that tapers rapidly. The thick bark is cinnamon-brown and peels in long strips. It is fire resistant. The yellow-green scales are keeled and glandular. The male flowers are yellow, 1/4" long, and carry abundant pollen in January. The female are yellow-green, scaly and grow at the branch ends. The elongate cones are light brown, 3/4"-1" long and have two seed leaves and a partition. There are two seeds in each half. The tree is used for incense in a small way, but mainly for fence posts, ties, shingles, pencils, chests and wardrobe linings.

Figure 87

55b Cone scales several. Fig. 88. ....
...........................WESTERN RED-CEDAR, *Thuja plicata* Donn

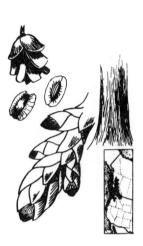

This conical-crowned tree grows up to 175' tall. The long, clear bole is widely buttressed at the base and tapers rapidly, the branches droop gracefully. The gray-brown bark is bright cinnamon underneath, shreds easily and is very inflammable. The dark green overlapping scales have a spicy odor, and are arranged in flat sprays in a fern-like pattern. The yellow male flowers are borne singly at the branch ends. The female are pink, also borne singly at branch ends, but very numerous. The mature cones are bud-like, 1/4"-1 1/2" long, with 6 flat, leathery scales. The seeds are double-winged. The wood is used for posts, poles, shingles, siding, doors and inside finish.

Figure 88

56a Leaves glandular, wood white. Fig. 89. ....
....PORT-ORFORD-CEDAR, *Chamaecyparis lawsoniana* Parl.

A conical-crowned tree, up to 200' tall, with a straight trunk and drooping branches. The thick bark is brown and forms long, loose, narrow fibers. The bright green leaf scales are glandular and the flat sprays are soft to touch. Male flowers are bright red; female, reddish brown. Cones are dark, reddish brown, berry-like, 1/2" in diameter, have 7 scales and stand erect on the upper branches. The wood has uses similar to Western Red-Cedar.

Figure 89

56b Wood bright yellow, strong offensive odor. Fig. 90. ....
............ALASKA-CEDAR, *Chamaecyparis nootkatensis* **Spach**

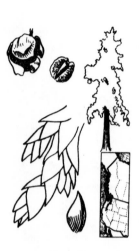

Also a coast tree, but more northerly, the Yellow-cedar grows up to 90′ tall, has an open, narrow, conical crown with wide-spaced, drooping branches. The trunk is often fluted and spiral. The ashy gray bark is mahogany brown inside and composed of long, thin scales. The blue-green leaf scales are sharp-pointed and prickly to touch. Male flowers are inconspicuous on the side branches. The female flowers are small, brown, erect cones near the end of the upper branches. The mature cones are deep, reddish brown, berry-like, 1/2″ in diameter, with whitish bloom and resin glands. There are 2-4 seeds under each scale. The bright yellow wood is used for boat building, interior finish, cabinet work and ornamental novelties. The wood has a very strong odor when sawn.

Figure 90

57a Trees columnar, cones elongate. Fig. 91. ....
PYRAMIDAL ARBORVITAE, *Thuja occidentalis pyramidalis*
Spaeth

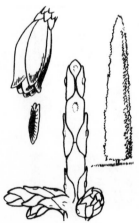

This variety of the Northern White-cedar is commonly planted around buildings in the west. It is pruned to a dense columnar shape and grows up to 40′ tall. The branches are short and horizontal. The brown cones are 1/2″ long and have from 6-10 clasping scales. Many other horticultural varieties are also planted. These trees are especially well adapted to lawn planting and formal landscaping because of the dense form and symmetrical neatness they assume when well kept and pruned.

Figure 91

57b Not as above **58**

58a Foliage in vertical fan shapes, cones with beaked scales. Fig.
92. ....ORIENTAL ARBORVITAE, *Thuja orientalis* L.

This is a small lawn tree, up to 60'
tall, with a dense foliage in fan-shaped
vertical sprays. The color of the leaves
varies from bright green to yellow-green
in the different varieties. The brown
cones have curved horns on each of the
6 leathery scales. It is native of China
and many ornamental varieties have
been developed.
—HIBA ARBORVITAE *Thujopsis dolo-*
brata is of Japanese origin. It is not quite
as tall as the above and has leaf scales
more than 3 times as large with silvery
patches below. The cones are more ball-
like and the horns are not as large or
recurved as in the Oriental Arborvitae.

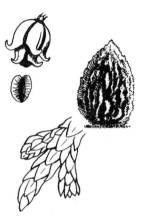

Figure 92

58b Not as above **59**

59a Leaves glandular, grows in northern California. Fig. 93. ....

....................MacNAB CYPRESS, *Cupressus macnabiana* **Murr.**

A bushy tree with an open crown, up
to 50' tall, greatly branched. The bark
is dark, reddish brown, scaly and in
ridges. The dark green leaf scales show
distinct resin glands. The male flowers
are cylindrical and appear at the branch
ends. The female are almost round. Mature cones are dark, reddish brown, ball-
like and hard. Each of the 6-8 scales has
a short, incurving horn. This tree is very
rare and grows at only a few scattered
places in the dry Sierra foothills from
Yuba county to the Oregon line.

Figure 93

59b Trees growing further south **60**

60a Tree straight and tapering, grows in Arizona and New Mexico. Fig. 94. ......ARIZONA CYPRESS, *Cupressus arizonica* **Greene**

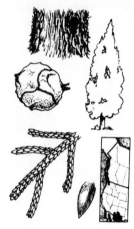

A straight, tapering tree with a conical crown, grows up to 80' tall and has a dense, pale foliage. The dark, reddish brown bark forms long loose scales. Pale green leaf scales are minute, overlapping and pointed. The flowers are yellow, inconspicuous and oblong. Mature cones are dark, reddish brown, 1" in diameter. They have 6-8 scales each with a central horn. This tree grows singly or in groups on the gravelly mountain slopes of the southwest and is valuable as ground cover to prevent erosion. Its wood is used for fuel and posts, but finds little other commercial use.

Figure 94

60b Trees more bushy, grows in central to southern California ..61

61a Low-spreading, contorted, found near Monterey Bay. Fig. 95. ....MONTEREY CYPRESS, *Cupressus macrocarpa* **Hart.**

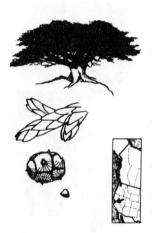

Weirdly shaped trees, up to 50' tall, with flat tops and long, twisted branches. The light, ashy gray bark is thin, hard and scaly. Dark yellow-green leaf scales with minutely toothed margins form a dense foliage. Male and female flowers occur on the same tree, but on different twigs. The tiny flowers are yellow and the female mature in 2 seasons into large cones 1 1/2" long, with 8-12 ashy brown scales. There are 15-20 seeds under each fertile scale. Because of the limited number of these trees and their deformed shape they would have little commercial use. They are protected and serve as a picturesque windbreak.

Figure 95

61b Growing beyond 2 miles of the Monterey Coast 62

62a Leaf scales without resin glands, cones almost smooth, seeds reddish brown. Fig. 96. ....
........................**SARGENT CYPRESS,** *Cupressus sargentii* **Jeps.**

A low, bushy tree, up to 30′ tall, with an open crown. The bark is dark, grayish brown and has narrow ridges and long scales. The dark green leaf scales turn bright red before dropping. Male flowers are minute, scaly and yellow. The female flowers are round and reddish. Mature cones are reddish brown to purple, 1/2″-1″ in diameter, in dense clusters and have only minute projections rather than horns. This rare tree grows on the dry mountain slopes of the counties around the San Francisco Bay area.

(This species is now considered a synonym of *C. goveniana* Gord.)

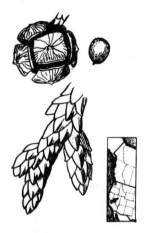

Figure 96

62b Cones smaller than above, seeds black. Fig. 97. ....
........................**GOWEN CYPRESS,** *Cupressus goveniana* **Gord.**

Usually a small tree, up to 40′ tall, but sometimes much taller. It has a wide, open, irregular crown with many branches. The bark is dull reddish brown and broken into a network of firm diagonal ridges. The dark green leaf scales are pointed. The cones are shiny and light brown with up to 20 black to brown seeds under each scale.

—DWARF CYPRESS, *C. pygmaea* Sarg. A dwarf form of *C. goveniana* is recognized by some as a distinct species since it has whip-like leading shoots.

—TECATE CYPRESS, *Cupressus guadalupensis* S. Wats. is a rare species of San Diego and Orange counties, characterized by shedding its bark and exposing a smooth reddish inner bark.

Figure 97

63a Fruit berry-like, Needles awl-like in whorls of 3. Fig. 98. ....
............................COMMON JUNIPER, *Juniperus communis* L.

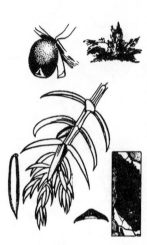

Usually a shrub with prostrate branches, but occasionally a tree, up to 20' tall. The bark is dark, reddish brown, in papery scales. The dark, bluish–green needles are chalky white above, pointed and very prickly to touch. Male and female flowers are borne on different trees. Both are small and inconspicuous. The berry-like fruit is bluish black, has a whitish bloom. Cone scales project out of the flesh at the flower end. It contains 2-3 seeds. The wood is used for turning, and the tree is sometimes used ornamentally.

—IRISH JUNIPER, *Juniperus communis hibernica* Gord. is a narrow, erect, small tree that is very popular for lawn planting.

Figure 98

63b Needles scale-like ....…..................64

64a Berry containing only 1 seed, leaf scales long and pointed. Fig. 99. ONE-SEED JUNIPER, *Juniperus monosperma* Sarg.

A slender-branched tree, up to 50' tall, with a trunk that may be 8"-10" in diameter. The bark is thin, ashy gray. The leaves are scale-like to awl-like, yellow-green, and may be quite spiny on older twigs. The small, inconspicuous flowers are found, male and female on different trees. The bluish black berries usually contain only one seed. The Indians found use for the bark by weaving it into mats, and ate the berries for food. The wood is used for posts and fuel.

Figure 99

64b Berries usually containing more than one seed 65

66a Scales in 4's, twigs 4-sided. Fig. 100. ....
ROCKY MOUNTAIN JUNIPER, *Juniperus scopulorum* **Sarg.**

A scrubby-looking tree, up to 40' tall, with branches long and erect, twigs drooping. The grayish bark is red-brown within, stringy and shredding in flakes. The dark gray-green scales are pointed and on larger branches are lengthened and even spiny. A slight gland can be seen near the tips of the scales. The flowers are minute and inconspicuous. The blackish blue berries have a pale bloom, are smooth, abundant, 1/4" in diameter, and 2-3 seeded. The red wood is used for fence posts. It is fine-grained and durable. Sudworth suggests it could be used for pencils.

Figure 100

66b Scales in 3's, twigs rounded, seeds pitted. Fig. 101. ....
.....................SIERRA JUNIPER, *Juniperus occidentalis* **Hook.**

A tree with an open, round-topped crown, up to 60' tall, trunk thick, divided near the base, branch tips turned up. The light cinnamon-brown bark is firm, stringy, thick and wide-furrowed. The scales are pale ashy green, overlapping and glandular. The inconspicuous flowers have the two sexes on different trees. Bluish black berries, covered with whitish bloom are 1/4" in diameter and have 2-3 seeds. The wood is used for posts, turning, cedar chests and pencils. It is fine-grained and exceedingly durable.

Figure 101

67a Bark in long, narrow shreds 68

67b Bark in small square plates. Fig. 102. ....
................ALLIGATOR JUNIPER, *Juniperus deppeana* Steud.

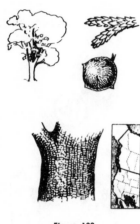

Figure 102

A heavy-trunked tree, up to 60' tall, with a trunk up to 5' thick, main branches heavy, often twisted due to its high mountain habitat. The bark differs from all other American junipers in that it is broken into flat-topped, square plates. It is dark, reddish brown to gray and 1"-4" thick. The pale blue-green leaves range from scale-like to awl-like, and the branches are covered with dense foliage. The flowers are inconspicuous, but male and female are on the same trees, unlike other junipers. The round, berry-like cone is 1/2" in diameter, dull red-brown, covered with a whitish bloom. It contains 4 seeds and a mealy pulp. The light yellow wood is close-grained and durable; it is used for posts but has little other commercial use because of its inaccessibility.

68a (abc) Low-spreading tree of the high deserts, seed pointed. Fig. 103. ....UTAH JUNIPER, *Juniperus osteosperma* Little

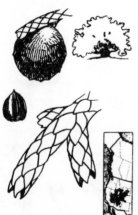

Figure 103

The short trunk of this tree divides into many low, spreading branches near the base making it quite bushy. It grows up to 12' tall. The trunk is fissured and twisted and the branches often distorted. The bark is light, ashy gray, in long thin scales. The pale yellow-green leaves are small, scale-like and overlapping. Small flowers are axillary with male and female on different trees. The reddish brown berry-like cone is covered with whitish bloom, usually contains one seed that is pointed and angled. The tree is too scrubby to be of any commercial use.

68b Tree taller, seed not pointed, trunk greatly fluted. Fig. 104.
.............CALIFORNIA JUNIPER, *Juniperus californica* **Carr.**

A round-topped tree, up to 30' tall, with a thick, fluted trunk and large twisted branches. The ashy gray bark has long fibrous scales. The leaf scales are pale yellow-green and overlapping. Male and female flowers are small, axillary, male and female on different trees. The light, reddish brown, berry-like cones are 1/4"-3/4" in diameter. Each cone has 2 angular, grooved seeds. The wood is used for turning, ornamental woodwork, posts and fuel. Indians eat the fruit. Green juniper berries yield the oil of juniper which is used as a diuretic in medicine.

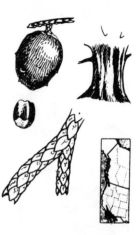

Figure 104

—PINCHOT JUNIPER, *J. pinchoti* Sudw. has red fruit half as large as *J. californica*, and scale-like leaves that are glandularly pitted.

68c Fruit a capsule, seeds numerous, leaves scale-like. TAMARISK
....page 62

BANANA, PALMS, YUCCAS

1a Trunk columnar, unbranched 2

1b Trunk may have a few branches 6

2a Leaves fan-like, fruit berry-like 3

2b Leaves pinnate 4

3a Trunk heavy, dead leaves hang down on trunk. Fig. 105. ....CALIFORNIA WASHINGTONIA, *Washingtonia filifera* H. Wendel.

The only native palm in our area grows in sheltered, spring-fed canyons of the Colorado and Mohave deserts. It is straight, up to 70′ tall, with a broad round top. The dead leaves hang to the ground, covering the whole trunk on a normal tree. On most planted trees they are pruned or else burned off by naughty boys who want fireworks. Even desert trees are very often mutilated in this way. The bark is dull, reddish brown, ribbed and fibrous. The pale green, fan-like leaves have the fibrous rays divided almost to the petiole. The rays are 4 1/2′ long, the petiole 5′-6′ long and armed with thorns. The small, white, perfect flowers are borne in branched clusters in the crown of the tree. They develop into small, black, elliptical berries, each containing one seed. The tree is used for street ornament. The wood is of no value.

Figure 105

3b Trunk slender, increasing in diameter from the base. Fig. 106. ....WINDMILL PALM, *Trachycarpus excelsa* Wendel.

A slender tree, up to 30′ tall, with a small trunk diameter at the base that is apparently increased toward the top by the heavy leaf stumps and intertwined fibers. Leaves are 2′-4′ across and petioles with rounded knobs are 2′-3′ long. The fruit is a small 3-lobed, violet colored drupe. This is a hardy Chinese palm that grows in most of California.

—CABBAGE PALMETTO, *Sabal palmetto* Lodd. is the Florida palm with yellow blossoms and black berries. It is planted in much of the west, especially in Texas and New Mexico.

Figure 106

4a Leaves with numerous slender leaflets 5

4b Leaves large, entire, but irregularly split 8

5a Fruit a date or berry-like. Fig. 107. ....
....DATE, *Phoenix dactylifera* L.

This is a straight-trunked tree, up to
70' tall with a dense crown of feathery
leaves. A native of the Southern Mediterranean it is grown extensively in the
Imperial Valley of California for its
fruit. It is also planted in parks as a
shade tree at times.

Figure 107

—CANARY ISLAND DATE PALM,
Phoenix canariensis Chaub. This heavy-
trunked tree has leaf blades up to 20'
long and grows to be 50' tall. Its dates
are orange-yellow and inedible but the
tree is hardy and is grown widely as a
street and park tree in most of California and Arizona.

5b Fruit a nut. Fig. 108. ....PLUME PALM, *Cocos plumosa* Hook.

This commonly grown tree is related
to the coconut palms. It has a smooth,
slender trunk and grows up to 40' tall.
The leaves are 10'-15' long, the flowers
are creamy and the fruits are orange-
colored nuts 1" long. It is a native of
Brazil.

Figure 108

—PINDO PALM, *Cocos australis* Mart.
This is the Paraguayan species of feather
palm. It grows about half as tall as the
Plume Palm and has stiff, gray-green
leaves. The nuts are edible.

6a Fruit a pod with numerous seeds 7

6b Fruit a berry. Fig. 109. ....
................................**GREEN DRACENA,** *Cordyline australis* **Hook.**

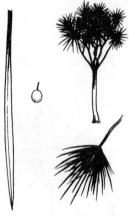

A small tree, up to 40′ tall, somewhat similar to the yuccas, but with a much more slender stem. Dull green leaves are 2′-3′ long. It has fragrant white flowers in erect or drooping panicles. The fruit is a white berry. This New Zealand tree is planted in California parks.

—DRAGON TREE, *Dracaena draco* L. A similar tree, up to 60′ tall, with orange colored berries. Introduced from the Canary Islands. Gets its name from the dried sap which is supposed to look like dragon's blood.

Figure 109

7a Leaves with shreddy filaments, seed pod round-tipped. Fig. 110.
................................**MOHAVE YUCCA,** *Yucca mohavensis* **Sarg.**

This tree grows up to 12′ tall and is not very often branched. The bark is dark brown, but mostly covered with a thatch of dead spines. The yellowish green, dagger-like leaves are 16″-24″ long and the margins have shredded filaments attached. The flowers are white, in a large, erect terminal spike. The fruit is a tan-colored capsule, 3-chambered, 3″-4″ long, has a rounded end, and contains numerous black seeds.
The two following Yuccas are closely related to the Mohave Yucca:

—SCHOTTS YUCCA, *Y. schottii*
Engelm.
This species of southern Arizona and Mexico has entire leaves. The shreddy filaments are missing.

Figure 110

—SOAPTREE YUCCA, *Y. elata* Engelm. This species has thin, flat leaves and long-stalked flower clusters. It is found in the same area as the above and also farther east.

7b Leaves finely toothed, shorter, seed pod pointed. Fig. 111. ....
....JOSHUA TREE, *Yucca brevifolia* **Engelm.**

A shaggy, branched tree, up to 25′ tall, with heads of spiny leaves. The ashy gray bark is cross-hatched, ridged and corky, but most of it is covered with a mat of spiny leaves. The bluish green leaves, 6″-10″ long, are bayonet-like, have finely-toothed margins and form dense clusters at the branch ends. The flowers are white, waxy-petaled, perfect, but foul smelling, in erect terminal clusters. The fruit is a pale brown capsule, 6-chambered, fleshy when green, pointed at the end and contains numerous black seeds. Yuccas have found little commercial use, but they provide nesting places for desert birds, and food for various desert animals, chief of which is probably the packrat.

Figure 111

—*Y. b. jaegeriana* McKelvey is a variety characterized by shorter leaves and a different manner of branching. It makes up the most extensive and dense portion of the yucca forest.

8 Fruit a banana. Fig. 112. ....
........COMMON BANANA, *Musa paradisiaca sapientum* **Kuntze**

Though actually not a tree, but a large perennial herb, it grows up to 25′ tall and since it is often mistaken for a tree it is included here. The leaves are enormous, 5′-10′ long, veins are pinnate and parallel. Leaf blades are often broken between veins. These are the edible bananas that are usually sold in stores. Bananas are not grown commercially in the United States but are often planted as curiosities in the southern part of California and do reasonably well. They are native to India.

Figure 112

THE BROADLEAFS

1a Leaves scale-like. Fig. 113. ....
.........SMALLFLOWER TAMARISK, *Tamarix parviflora* DC.

A small tree up to 20' feet tall with minute, deciduous, scale-like leaves, pink flowers in raceme-like clusters and fruit capsules with numerous seeds. This is a Southern European tree but has escaped from cultivation in southern California and is commonly seen along river beds in alkali soils.

—*Tamarix articulata* Vahl. is also common in the south. This is the evergreen species. It grows up to 35' tall and also has pink flowers. It is used as a windbreak and is common in the Imperial Valley and along the southern coastline.

Figure 113

1b Leaves not scale-like 2

2a Leaves succulent, spiny, minute, or absent. CACTI ....page 127

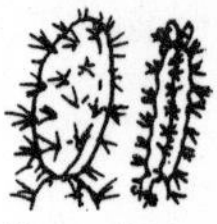

Figure 114

2b Leaves not as above 3

3a Leaves simple. Fig. 115. 4

3b Leaves compound. Fig. 116. ......
....page 129   Figure 115    Figure 116

4a Fruit a catkin. POPLARS, COTTONWOODS and WILLOWS
....page 64

4b Fruit not a catkin, blossoms may be on one 5

5a Fruit a nut. OAKS and FILBERTS ....page 82

5b Fruit other than above 6

6a Fruit a small woody cone. ALDERS. ....page 80

Figure 117

6b Fruit not cone-like 7

7a Fruit berry-like ....page 90

7b Fruit other than berry-like 8

8a Seed with feathery tail attached. CERCOCARPUS and CLIFF-
ROSE ....page 121

8b Seed not as above 9

9a Catkin bracts 3-lobed, bark peels horizontally. BIRCHES ....
.... page 78

9b Fruit not as above 10

10a Fruit drupe-like, containing one seed. AVOCADO, PLUM,
CHERRY ....page 100

10b Fruit not as above 11

11a Fruit a capsule containing seeds ....page 111

11b Fruit not as above 12

12a Fruit a pome. APPLES, PEARS and QUINCES ....page 106

12b Fruit not as above 13

13a Fruit compound or an aggregate. MULBERRY, OSAGE-
ORANGE, and FIG ....page 109

13b Fruit other than above 14

14a Fruit a legume type pod. Figure 118.
....page 134

Figure 118

14b Fruit other than above 15

15a Fruit a winged seed. Figure 119.
....page 121

Figure 119

15b Fruit other than above 16

16a Fruit a citrocarp. ORANGE, GRAPEFRUIT, LEMON, etc.
....page 108

16b Fruit a woody cone. MAGNOLIA and YELLOW-POPLAR
....page 110

POPLARS AND WILLOWS

1a Trees erect, bark white to gray, leaves generally broad and long-stemmed. POPLARS 2

1b Trees often shrubby, trunks multiple, leaves usually narrow and often sessile, bark green to brown. WILLOWS 9

2a Petioles flattened 3

2b Petioles rounded...7

3a Bark gray-green to white 4

3b Bark gray to brown, thick and furrowed 5

4a Leaves large toothed, snow-white underneath. Fig. 120. ....
....WHITE POPLAR, *Populus alba* L.

This tree with a bark similar to that of the aspen is heavier and grows up to 70′ tall. The branches are heavy and the extensive root system sprouts vigorously. The silvery white under side of the leaves shows up strongly in a wind. It has been introduced from Southern Europe and is fairly common in the west.

Figure 120

4b Leaves round and greenish underneath. Fig. 121. ....
..........................QUAKING ASPEN, *Populus tremuloides* Michx.

A slender-trunked tree up to 80′ tall, with a narrow, irregular crown. The bark is yellow-green with a white bloom and dark branch scars. The smooth, thin, outside layer is papery. The dark green leaves are round, with a pointed tip. Having a petiole that is long and flat, the leaves tremble in the slightest breeze. The red-gray drooping catkins are up to 4″ long. Male and female are found on different trees. The mature female catkin is made of light green capsules packed full of very small brown seeds. The white wood is used for pulp, boxes, excelsior, fuel and matches. This tree is the favorite food of the beaver.

Figure 121

Indians burned it when in enemy territory because it gave off very little smoke.

5a Tree shape columnar, branches ascending. Fig. 122. ....
..............**LOMBARDY POPLAR,** *Populus nigra italica* **Muench.**

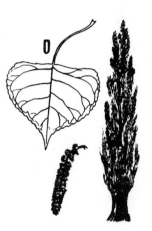

This rapidly growing tree can be recognized at a great distance by its columnar shape. The trunk is short, heavy and covered with suckers, branches are large and erect. Shiny, bright green leaves have flattened petioles. Since it is propagated from shoots and only male trees have been imported from its native Italy this tree does not produce the downy seeds common to the genus. It is commonly planted along fence rows and does things to a landscape.
—CAROLINA POPLAR, *Populus canadensis* Muench. This tree also has only staminate catkins in its introduced form and does not scatter down in the spring. It is a favorite for park planting in the northern states and Canada.

Figure 122

5b Trees more spreading 6

6a Seed capsule acutely pointed. Fig. 123. ....
..................**PLAINS COTTONWOOD,** *Populus sargentii* **Dode**

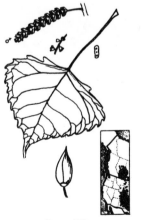

A broad open-crowned tree up to 90′ tall. The bark is pale gray, thick, deeply grooved, in rounded ridges. The light green leaves are shiny and have flattened stems. The male catkins are short, 2″-2 1/2″ long, the female on different trees are 4″-8″ long at maturity. The individual capsules are tapered, pointed and nearly 1/2″ long. This large shade tree is usually found growing along streams in the plains region. It is useful for fuel and erosion control.

Figure 123

6b Seed capsule more obtuse. Fig. 124. ....
........**FREMONT COTTONWOOD,** *Populus fremontii* **S. Wats.**

A crooked-trunked tree, up to 90′ tall with heavy limbs. The dark, grayish brown bark is red inside, rough and deeply furrowed. The yellow-green leaves are shiny, smooth, leathery and thick. Male and female catkins are found on separate trees. Mature capsules are not as acutely pointed as in *P. sargentii*. They are full of seeds and abundant down. The tree is used locally for fuel and erosion control. It is quite similar to the eastern tree *P. deltoides* that barely extends into the range covered by this book in northern Montana and Alberta.

—RIO GRANDE COTTONWOOD, *Populus fremontii wislizenii* S. Wats. It grows along the Rio Grande river.

Figure 124

—PARRY COTTONWOOD, *P. parryi* Sarg. has characteristics of the Fremont and Black Cottonwoods.

7a Leaves less than half as wide as long. Fig. 125. ....
NARROWLEAF COTTONWOOD, *Populus angustifolia* **James**

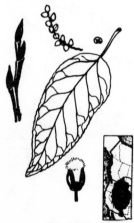

A more slender-limbed tree, up to 60′ tall, with a narrow, pyramidal crown. The bark, which is pale green on the limbs, is dark gray and fissured on the trunk. Yellow-green leaves are shiny above, pale below, lanceolate, and willow-like with the petioles rounded but a little flat above. The short-stalked catkins are dense with 12-20 stamens on each flower. The fruiting catkin is erect or partly so and the capsules are plump. It finds use for fuel and as a shade tree.

Figure 125

7b Leaves not as above 8

**8a Leaves tapered, seed capsules 3-valved and hairy. Fig. 126.
BLACK COTTONWOOD,** *Populus trichocarpa* **Torr. & Gray**

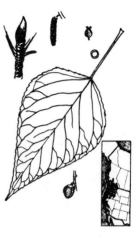

A clean-trunked tree, up to 125' tall, with a wide crown and erect branches. The pale gray bark is thick and deeply furrowed. The leaves are deep green, shiny above, whitish below, thick, leathery, smooth and have round petioles. Male and female flowers grow on separate trees. The male catkins are dense-flowered and have slender stems. The female flowers are farther apart and the stem of the catkin is heavier. The 3-valved capsule contains many downy seeds. The timber is used for veneer, strawberry boxes, planks for wine vats and cheese curing, barrels, boxes and fuel.

Figure 126

8b Seed capsules 2-valved, buds very sticky. Fig. 127. ....
.................................**BALSAM POPLAR,** *Populus balsamifera* **L.**

An erect-branching tree, up to 100' tall with a narrow, pyramidal crown. The bark is reddish gray to greenish gray and forms deep furrows and firm ridges. The dark green leaves are lustrous, paler below. Buds are large and sticky. The long-stalked male and female catkins come out on different trees before the leaves appear. Light green seed capsules are 2-valved and short-stalked. The wood is used for boxes, pulp, fuel and crating. The sticky buds find use in cough medicine.

Figure 127

THE WILLOWS

9a Stamens 1, twigs and under side of leaves covered with fine, silvery hair. Fig. 128. ....
....**SITKA WILLOW,** *Salix sitchensis* **Sanson**

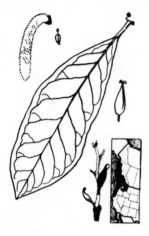

Usually a leaning tree, up to 12′ tall, trunk greatly branched, branches slender but crooked. The bark is reddish brown, thin and scaly. Twigs are minutely hairy. The deep green leaves are shiny above, covered with silky hairs below, 3″-5″ long. Catkins appear with the leaves and are 1 1/2″-3″ long, the flowers have 1 stamen. The fruit is a beaked, tapered capsule. Like most willows it is useful for erosion control and ground cover. —COULTER WILLOW, S. *coulteri* Anderss. Now listed as a full species. Found in Northern Idaho and surrounding states.

Figure 128

9b Stamens 2 or more **10**

10a Stamens 2 ....**11**

10b Stamens more than 2 ....**24**

11a Small twigs and under side of leaves coated with felt-like hair. Fig. 129. ....**FELTLEAF WILLOW,** *Salix alexensis* **Cov.**

Usually a shrubby tree but will grow up to 25′ tall. The bark is brown and firm-scaled, downy on twigs. The yellow-green leaves, 2 1/2″-4″ long, are densely coated on the under side with shiny white hair. The mid-vein is yellow. Flowers on the male catkins have 2 stamens. Hairy seed pods are in dense, erect clusters. This tree usually is found growing in gravel deposits along creek beds.

Figure 129

11b Under side of leaves not noticeably hairy **12**

12a Leaves small, 1″ long, linear lanceolate. Fig. 130. ....
............................YEWLEAF WILLOW, *Salix taxifolia* **H.B.K.**

A small tree, usually shrubby, up to 12′ tall. The bark is a pale greenish gray and scaly. The pale green leaves are lighter underneath, narrow, yew-like and much smaller than the leaves of most other willows. They are 1/2″-1 1/4″ long, linear to lanceolate. The flowers are found on short, thick catkins. The male flowers have 2 stamens. The fruit pods are beaked and tapered. This tree grows along stream beds and washes of the deserts in the Southwest. It helps prevent erosion in a country where that danger is great.

Figure 130

12b Leaves not exceptionally small **13**

13a Leaves exceptionally broad, young twigs hairy, Fig. 131. ......
............................YAKUTAT WILLOW, *Salix amplifolia* **Cov.**

This tree grows up to 25′ tall, has a branched trunk and irregular crown. The dark brown bark is scaly. The leaves are light yellow-green, smooth above, whitish below, petioles hairy, blades very broad, 2″-2 1/2″ long by 1″-1 1/2″ broad. The male flowers are found on catkins 1 1/2″-2″ long. The dark brown scales have long pale hairs and 2 stamens. The female flowers are shorter and stouter with a slender 2-lobed stigma. The mature fruiting catkin is short-stalked, rounded and has long-pointed, beaked pods. It is usually found growing on sand dunes along the Alaskan sea coast.

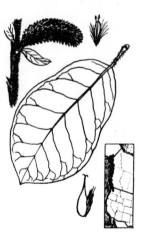

Figure 131

13b Leaves not exceptionally broad **14**

14a Leaves linear, often sessile **19**

14b Leaves not linear **15**

15a Leaf blades inclined to be widest toward the tip end **16**

15b Leaf blades not as above **17**

16a Leaves thin, smooth, and shiny. Fig. 132. ....
...........................SCOULER WILLOW, *Salix scouleriana* **Barr.**

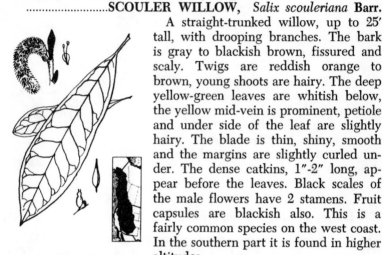

A straight-trunked willow, up to 25′ tall, with drooping branches. The bark is gray to blackish brown, fissured and scaly. Twigs are reddish orange to brown, young shoots are hairy. The deep yellow-green leaves are whitish below, the yellow mid-vein is prominent, petiole and under side of the leaf are slightly hairy. The blade is thin, shiny, smooth and the margins are slightly curled under. The dense catkins, 1″-2″ long, appear before the leaves. Black scales of the male flowers have 2 stamens. Fruit capsules are blackish also. This is a fairly common species on the west coast. In the southern part it is found in higher altitudes.

Figure 132

16b Leaves thick, seed pods long-beaked. Fig. 133. ....
....BEBB WILLOW, *Salix bebbiana* **Sarg.**

A shrubby tree, up to 25′ tall. The bark is thin, grayish green, reddish on twigs and whitish on new shoots. The dull green leaves are silvery white beneath with fine, rusty hairs. Male catkins yellowish, stamens 2. The mature fruiting capsules are brown with white hair. This willow grows in moist thickets along streams and is used for withes and erosion control. The Indians made fish-lines out of the stringy inner bark. Sometimes called Beaked Willow because of the long beaks on the fruiting pods.

Figure 133

17a Leaves thick, leathery, entire petiole and mid-vein bright yellow. Fig. 134. ....
.................................**ARROYO WILLOW,** *Salix lasiolepis* **Benth.**

This willow grows up to 30' tall, has slim branches that tend upward strongly and form an irregular crown. The bark is dark brown to blackish, in shallow seams and wide ridges. On young stems it is a smooth ash gray and on twigs a red brown. The dark yellow-green leaves are silvery white beneath, smooth above, thick and leathery, 2 1/2"-5 1/2" long, with a bright yellow petiole and mid-vein. The catkins are 1 1/4"-2 1/2" long and appear before the leaves come out. The fruiting capsules are beaked and pear-shaped. It grows in washes in the more arid parts of the Southwest. It is also called the White Willow.

Figure 134

17b Leaves serrate or finely toothed **18**

18a Leaf blades about half as wide as long, shoots and twigs hairy. Fig. 135. ....**HOOKER WILLOW,** *Salix hookeriana* **Barr.**

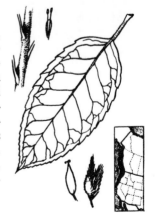

A multiple-trunked tree, up to 20' tall, but often quite shrubby. The pale, reddish brown bark is thin, scaly and indistinctly seamed, young branches are a red-brown, shoots and twigs are covered with a white wool. The shiny, yellow-green leaves are smooth above, mid-veins are hairy beneath. Male flowers have two stamens on the yellow scales. The fruiting capsule has a bilobed beak. This willow is often found near tidewater streams and salt marshes.

Figure 135

**18b Leaves one third as wide as long, petioles long. Fig. 136. ....
................MACKENZIE WILLOW,** *Salix mackenzieana* **Barr.**

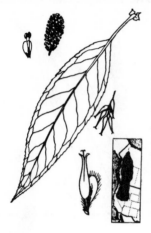

A slender, straight tree with a narrow crown. The ashy gray bark is thin and smooth. The deep olive leaves are paler beneath, 2"-3" long, smooth on both sides, mid-veins yellow. The male flowers have 2 stamens, female a 2-parted stigma. It grows along stream banks of the interior. The type was collected along the Mackenzie river and the tree was named in honor of Alexander Mackenzie the discoverer of the river.

Figure 136

**19a Leaf margins entire or nearly so. Fig. 137. ....
....HINDS WILLOW,** *Salix hindsiana* **Benth.**

This willow usually has a single stem and grows to be 20' tall. The bark is greenish brown and smooth, hairy on young twigs. The green leaves are pale beneath, smooth above and below, long and narrow, 2"-6" long. The catkins are sessile, the male flowers have 2 stamens. The fruit capsule is smooth, shiny and beaked. This tree is common along the river beds and washes from Oregon to Lower California. Useful for erosion control.

—SERVICEBERRY WILLOW, S. *padophylla* Rydb. Found on either side of the Rockies from Alaska to Colorado. Usually a shrub.

Figure 137

19b Leaf margins serrate or finely toothed 20

20a Leaves linear lanceolate, petioles short. Fig. 138. ....
............................SANDBAR WILLOW, *Salix interior* **Rowlee**

This tree is usually reed-like on sand-
bars, but in a permanent location it will
grow to be 50' tall. The grayish brown
bark has a faint reddish tinge. The
leaves are yellow-green above, paler below, smooth, 3"-5" long. Catkins are
short and thick, male flowers have 2
stamens. The fruiting capsule is light
brown, 1/4" long with a 2-parted beak.
This willow with its subspecies is much
used for basket and furniture weaving.

—GEYER WILLOW, *S. geyeriana* Anderss. grows from Montana to California. Usually a shrub, now listed as a
tree.

—TRACY WILLOW, *S. tracyi* Ball is
found in northwestern California and
southwestern Oregon.

Figure 138

—RIVER WILLOW, *S. fluviatilis* Nutt. found only on lower Columbia River Valley and adjacent areas.

20b Leaves sessile or nearly so ....…...**21**

21a Tree branches decidedly drooping. Fig. 139. ....
...................................WEEPING WILLOW, *Salix babylonica* **L.**

This beautiful tree with its character-
istically drooping branchlets is very
widely planted in the west both as a
lawn and park tree. Both the green-twig
and the yellow-twig varieties are common. It grows very rapidly and provides
a dense, humid shade.

—GOLDEN WILLOW, *Salix alba vitel-
lina* Stokes. This tree with bright yellow
twigs, but not the strongly "weeping"
habit is also widely planted in the northwest.

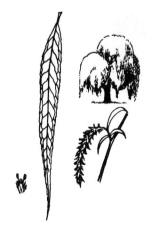

Figure 139

21b Trees not having noticeably drooping branches **22**

22a Twigs and mid-rib covered with fine hair. Fig. 140. ....
.... **NORTHWEST WILLOW,** *Salix sessilifolia* **Nutt.**

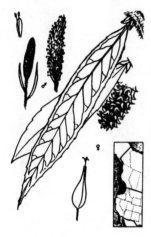

A tree similar to the Sandbar Willow, grows up to 25′ tall, slender. The grayish brown bark forms irregular seams. Young twigs have a grayish wool. The narrow, light pea-green leaves are smooth above, lightly covered with silky hairs beneath, mid-veins are lemon yellow. Male flowers have 2 stamens, the female has a 3-parted stigma. The fruiting capsule is slender-necked. This tree is also used for basketry purposes and Indian fish nets.

Figure 140

22b Twigs not noticeably hairy **23**

23a Twigs and leaves shiny, gray-green. Fig. 141. ....
...................................**COYOTE WILLOW,** *Salix exigua* **Nutt.**

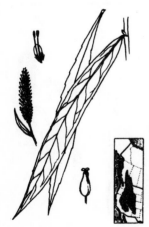

A shrub or small tree up to 20′ tall. The gray bark is rough and fissured on the trunk, but brown, shiny and smooth on the branches. The gray-green leaves are nearly sessille, 1″-5 1/2″ long, smooth above and silky-haired beneath. The yellow catkins appear with the leaves. Male flowers have 2 stamens, female a 2-lobed stigma. Fruiting capsules are smooth. It is only in Eastern Washington that this willow grows to tree size. A number of former subspecies are not listed in the 1953 check list.

Figure 141

23b Leaves dark green, margins finely toothed. Fig. 142. ....
.................................DUSKY WILLOW, *Salix melanopsis* **Nutt.**

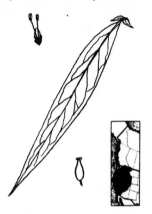

A shrub or tree up to 15' tall. The brownish gray bark is smooth, twigs are smooth except at the tip where they are woolly. Dark green leaves are paler beneath, 2"-4" long and smooth. The yellowish catkins are 1"-2 1/2" long by 1/2" wide, stamens 2. Fruiting capsule is smooth without hair. This tree gets its name from the dark brown to black twigs. Two subspecies, *bolanderiana* and *tenerrima* are no longer listed.

Figure 142

24a Leaves yellow-green on both sides. Fig. 143. ....
...........................WHIPLASH WILLOW, *Salix caudata* **Heller**

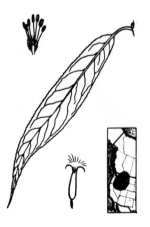

This tree grows up to 35' tall and is characterized by numerous long upright suckers. The smooth brown bark changes to chestnut on the branches which are also smooth and shiny. The yellow-green leaves are slightly paler beneath, 1 1/2"-3" long and smooth. The yellowish catkins appear with the leaves, stamens number 5-7. Stigmas are lobed. The fruiting capsule is 1/2" long and smooth. The long straight suckers of this tree were useful for buggy whips to an earlier generation, probably also had something to do with forming the character of this one.

Figure 143

24b Leaves whitish below **25**

25a Petioles having warty glands near the blade. Fig. 144. ....
..PACIFIC WILLOW, *Salix lasiandra* **Benth.**

Figure 144

A tree with a clear, crooked trunk, up to 30′ tall having straight vertical branches and an unsymmetrical crown. The dark brown bark is broken into flat plates. Twigs are yellow to brown. The dark yellow-green leaves are whitish below, 4 1/2″-5″ long, shiny above, smooth beneath, mid-veins are orange-yellow, warty glands appear on the petiole near the leaf blade. Catkins, 1 1/4″-3″ long, appear with and after the leaves, stamens 5-9. Tree grows on the banks of rivers and streams.

25b Petioles not as above 26

26a Leaves blue-green, branches orange to red-brown. Fig. 145.
..RED WILLOW, *Salix laevigata* **Bebb**

Figure 145

Generally single-stemmed, up to 40′ tall with a broad, round-topped crown. The dark, reddish brown bark is roughly furrowed with firm, narrow ridges. Twigs are orange. The blue-green leaves are whitish below, smooth throughout, 3 1/2″-6 1/2″ long and finely serrulate, mid-veins are yellow. The showy catkins are 1 1/4″-4″ long, peduncled and often bent. The wood is a pale, reddish brown.

26b Not as above 27

27a Leaves pale yellow-green, smooth above and below. Fig. 146.
....................................GOODING WILLOW, *Salix goodingii* **Ball**

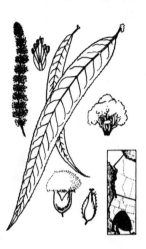

A tree with multiple trunks, up to 40′ tall. The trunks are crooked and bowed and form a wide, round-topped crown. The furrowed bark is blackish brown on the trunk to yellow on the branchlets. Pale green leaves, 2 1/2″-4″ long are smooth above and below. Catkins 1 1/2″-2 1/2″ long appear with the leaves. The fruit is a pointed capsule. The pale, reddish brown wood is used for charcoal, firewood and fence pickets.

Figure 146

27b Leaves not as above 28

28a Twigs bright yellow, as alpine tree. Fig. 147. ....
....YELLOW WILLOW, *Salix lutea* **Nutt.**

This is an erect tree up to 60′ tall with dark purplish brown bark and bright yellow twigs and grows in high altitudes. The leaves are dark green above, paler beneath, finely serrate and shiny. Catkins have 5-9 stamens. Fruit is light, reddish brown. This tree grows along streams in the high mountains.

—STRAPLEAF WILLOW, *S. ligulifolia* Ball usually a shrub, now listed as a tree. Grows from California to Montana.

Figure 147

28b Leaves ovate lanceolate, light green above, pale beneah. Fig. 148. ....PEACHLEAF WILLOW, *Salix amygdaloides* Anderss.

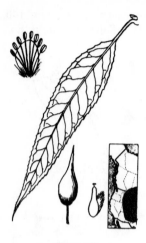

This willow grows to be up to 40′ tall in the west, has a straight or leaning trunk and a compact round head. The pale, reddish brown bark is deeply furrowed. Twigs are yellow to orange-brown. The shiny yellow-green leaves are whitish and smooth beneath and have prominent yellow mid-veins. Catkins, 2″-3″ long, appear with the leaves. They are peduncled, have 5-9 stamens and a 2-parted stigma. The fruiting capsule is pointed and smooth.

—BONPLAND WILLOW, *S. bonplandiana* H.B.K. is a species similar to the Peachleaf but with short-stalked capsules. It occurs in the southern portions of the western states bordering Mexico.

Figure 148

BIRCHES AND ALDERS

1a Fruit borne in a catkin-like, disintegrating cone with 3-lobed scales 2

1b Fruit not as above 4

2a Bark separates easily into papery layers 3

2b Bark dark bronze, not easily separated into layers. Fig. 149. ....WATER BIRCH, *Betula occidentalis* Hook.

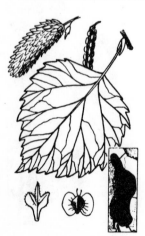

A slender-stemmed tree up to 25′ tall with a thin crown. The bark is dark, copper colored, shiny, twigs are green and have glandular dots. Fruiting catkins are erect, seeds small, 2-winged. The tree is used for fuel and to conserve moisture and prevent erosion.

—PIPER WATER BIRCH *B. o. fecunda* Fern. is found in eastern Washington, has longer and narrower cone.

—YUKON BIRCH, *Betula eastwoodiae* Sarg. is found in northern British Columbia, Yukon and eastern Alaska.

—HORNE BIRCH, *B, hornei* But. is found in central and southern Alaska.

Figure 149

3a Bark white to brown, peels horizontally into thin layers. Fig. 150. ....
......WESTERN PAPER BIRCH, *Betula papyrifera commutata* Fern.

This graceful tree grows up to 90' tall in the west and has an open, round-topped crown. The bark peels easily, is smooth, shiny and varies in color from white to light yellow orange to brown. The dull deep green leaves are yellowish green beneath, 2 1/2"-3 1/2" long with a yellow mid-vein. Fruiting catkins are erect, seeds 2-winged. The wood makes excellent fuel and is also used for veneer.

—NORTHWESTERN PAPER BIRCH, *B. p. subcordata* Sarg. found in the northwest differs from the species chiefly in the shape and toothing of the leaves.

—KENAI PAPER BIRCH *B. p. kenaica* Henry occurs along the coast of Alaska. It has dark brown furrowed bark and is rare.

Figure 150

—ALASKA PAPER BIRCH, *B. p. humilis* Fern. & Raup. occurs in Alaska and northern British Columbia to Saskatchewan.

3b Branchlets drooping, leaves deeply lobed. Fig. 151. ....
........CUTLEAF EUROPEAN BIRCH, *Betula pendula gracilis* Rehd.

A graceful, white-barked tree with erect trunk and spreading branches with drooping branchlets. The leaves are deeply cut and narrowly pointed. Winged seeds grow in short catkins or cone-like structures. These trees are commonly planted on lawns and streets and are fairly hardy but subject to insect damage.

—EUROPEAN WHITE BIRCH, *B. alba* L. This tree in its varied horticultural varieties is quite widely planted.

—GRAY BIRCH, *B. populifolia* Marsh. also has many ornamental varieties that are popular for lawn and roadside planting.

Figure 151

4a Fruit a two-winged nutlet in a woody cone, a strobile. AL-DERS 5

4b Fruit a wingless seed in a hop-like cone. Fig. 152. ....
.........**KNOWLTON HOPHORNBEAM,** *Ostrya knowltonii* **Cov.**

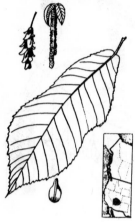

A tree up to 30′ tall with long slender branches. The bark is thickly furrowed in narrowed grooves by scales that are tight in the center and raised at the edges. The leaves are thin and transparent. They have short petioles and are slightly heart-shaped at the petiole. The catkins are slender and the fruit hop-like. These trees are found in only a small area on the Colorado river about 70 miles north of Flagstaff, Arizona.

Figure 152

5a Seed wings very narrow, cones small. Fig. 153. ....
....**WHITE ALDER,** *Alnus rhombifolia* **Nutt.**

A tree with straight, clear stems, up to 75′ tall, with a broad, open, dome-like crown. The brown bark is thin and scaly. The light yellow-green leaves are fine toothed, have wavy edges and a yellow mid-vein. The catkins, 4 1/2″-5 1/2″ long, flower in midwinter. The cones are 1/2″-3/4″ long, they shed their seeds in winter. The seeds have a very narrow wing. The wood is used for fuel and cabinet work. It must be sawn immediately after cutting, otherwise the wood will be discolored.

Figure 153

5b Seed wings wider **6**

6a Seed wings as large as the seed, flowering in spring. Fig. 154.
....**SITKA ALDER,** *Alnus sinuata* **Rydb.**

A small, slender tree, up to 10′ tall, with short horizontal branches and a narrow crown. The dull, bluish gray bark is thin and smooth. Yellow-green leaves are lighter below, thin, papery and smooth. Male catkins are 3″-5″ long, bloom in the spring. Cones are 1/2″-3/4″ long, seeds minute, gauzy-winged. It forms forest cover in the moist areas of the western states to Alaska.

Figure 154

6b Seed wings smaller, flowering in winter or early spring **7**

7a Bark pale gray, patchy, grows in coastal lowlands. Fig. 155.
....**RED ALDER,** *Alnus rubra* **Bong.**

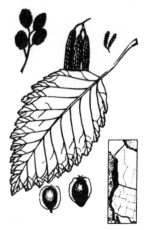

A straight-trunked tree, up to 90′ tall, narrow, dome-like crown. The thin, smooth bark is ashy gray changing to mahogany red on the glandular twigs. The deep yellow-green leaves are paler beneath, 2″-6″ long, smooth above with short, rusty hairs on the veins underneath. Male catkins are 5″-6″ long, fruiting cones are 1/2″-1″ long. Cone scales are thickened at the ends, blunt and square. The wood of this tree is used for fuel and furniture making.

Figure 155

7b Bark reddish brown, grows in higher altitudes. Fig. 156. ....
........................THINLEAF ALDER, *Alnus tenuifolia* **Nutt.**

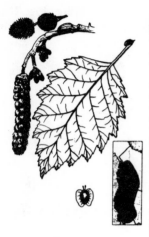

A slender tree with bent stems, up to 25′ tall with a narrow, dome-like crown. The dark, grayish brown bark is scaled and reddish on heavy trunks, but usually thin and smooth. The leaves are deep grass-green, 2″-4″ long, thin, smooth above, lighter below, petiole and midvein yellow. The male catkins are 2″-3″ long and open in early spring. This tree grows along streams in slightly higher altitudes than the Red Alder. It is of little commercial use.

—ARIZONA ALDER, *Alnus oblongifolia* Torr. is found in southern Arizona and New Mexico and is characterized by leaves that are not doubly serrate.

Figure 156

FILBERT, CHINKAPIN AND OAKS

1a Fruit a twin nut with tailed husks. Fig. 157. ....
..................................GIANT FILBERT, *Corylus maxima* **Mill.**

This bushy tree grows up to 30′ tall and has smooth gray bark and hairy, glandular twigs. The leaves are 3″-4″ long, dark green, hairy on both sides. Flowers come in pendulous catkins with conspicuous red styles. The paired nuts are covered with a hairy, fringed case. These are the commercial filberts or hazel nuts. They are grown in all the Pacific states and southern British Columbia.

—CALIFORNIA HAZEL *Corylus cornuta californica* grows to tree size in California.

Figure 157

1b Nut other than above **2**

2a Fruit a spiny bur that contains 4 nuts. Fig. 158. ....
........**GOLDEN CHINKAPIN,** *Castanopsis chrysophylla* **A. DC.**

A heavy-limbed tree, up to 100' tall with a dense crown that is pyramidal to dome-shaped. The bark is reddish brown, bright red within, thick, deeply furrowed between wide plates. The evergreen leaves are shiny, olive-green above, yellow beneath, thick, leathery, 2 1/2"-3 1/2" long. The male and female flowers are borne on different trees. They are inconspicuous and open in early spring. A spiny bur, 1"-1 3/4" in diameter usually contains 4 shiny, yellow-brown nuts that are sweet and edible. The wood is used for implement handles.

Figure 158

2b Nut an acorn **3**

3a Acorns mature in two seasons, leaves usually with sharp points
....**4**

3b Acorns mature in one season, leaves usually round-lobed **8**

4a Male blossoms erect, leaves pinnately parallel-veined. Fig. 159.
.....................................**TANOAK,** *Lithocarpus densiflorus* **Rehd.**

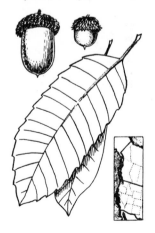

A tree, up to 80' tall with a trunk that is usually short and crooked, branches wide, horizontal, crown broad. The pale brown bark is blotched with grayish areas, thick and firm with deep, narrow seams and square-shaped plates. The light green leaves are smooth and shiny with reddish hairs on the veins beneath. They remain on the tree for 3-4 seasons. Male flowers are in erect catkins that are thicker than oak flowers, female are in clusters. The acorns mature in 2 years, are pale yellow-brown, 3/4"-1" long, cup scales bristly. The bark is used for tanning and the wood for implements and furniture.

Figure 159

4b Male blossom a pendulous catkin, cup scales clasping. BLACK
OAKS **5**

5a Leaves deciduous **6**

5b Leaves remaining on tree at least till spring **7**

6a Leaves deeply lobed, sharp pointed, Pacific coast tree. Fig. 160.
.............CALIFORNIA BLACK OAK, *Quercus kelloggii* Newb.

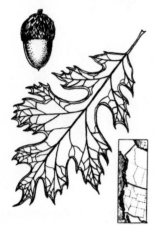

A tree up to 80′ tall with bent, leaning trunk and broad, open crown. The bark is blackish brown, hard, rough and deeply furrowed. The thick, shiny leaves are deep olive above, paler and hairy beneath, deciduous. Pale chestnut acorns, 1″-1 1/4″ long, are half concealed by the cup and are downy at the apex. They remain on the tree for 2 seasons. The wood is used for fuel and the bark for tanning.

Figure 160

6b Leaves not deeply lobed, tips pointed, grows in Arizona and
New Mexico. Fig. 161. ....EMORY OAK, *Quercus emoryi* Torr.

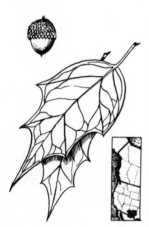

This is a more scrubby tree found east of the Rockies, up to 50′ tall, short-trunked with wide spreading branches and a rounded crown. The bark is dark gray, rough, thick and furrowed. The yellow-green leaves are not often lobed but have few large teeth and an acuminate tip. Male flowers are in pendant racemes, female are basal on twigs of the previous year. The acorns remain on the tree for two seasons. They may be in pairs or else single. The heartwood of this tree is almost black, the sapwood is reddish in color. The wood is used mainly for fuel since the short crooked trunk does not supply the best saw logs.

Figure 161

7a Leaves bristle tipped, acorns pointed. Fig. 162. ....
........................**INTERIOR LIVE OAK,** *Quercus wislizenii* **A. DC.**

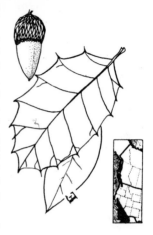

This tree is not as enormous as the California Live Oak, but grows to be 75' tall. Stout, spreading branches form a rounded crown. The grayish bark is rough and furrowed. Deep green leaves are shiny above, yellow-green beneath, leathery and smooth. The petioles are hairy and the blades can be distinguished from *Q. agrifolia* in that they are flat and seldom curled. They remain on the tree 2 seasons. The acorn is long and slender, 1"-1 1/2" long, and the cup scales are long and reddish brown. The acorns take 2 years to mature. Wood is used for fuel.

—ORACLE OAK, *Quercus moreha* Kellogg seems to be a cross between the Interior Live Oak and the California

Figure 162

Black Oak. The leaves are similar to *Q. wislizenii* and are shed from midwinter to spring. The nuts are heavy and take 2 seasons to mature.

7b Acorn cups covered with fine yellow hair. Fig. 163. ....
....................**CANYON LIVE OAK,** *Quercus chrysolepis* **Liebm.**

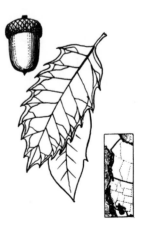

A short-trunked tree, up to 50' tall with wide-spreading branches that sometimes give it a round-topped crown up to 100' across. The bark is soft and scaly, light gray to dark reddish brown on the twigs. The thick leathery leaves are shiny, yellow-green above, hairy beneath, evergreen. They vary greatly in size and shape. Some are entire, others have many sharp teeth. The pale chestnut acorns mature in 2 seasons and are downy at the tip. The wood is used for implements and firewood.

—PALMER OAK, *Q. c. palmeri* Sarg. is found in Arizona, New Mexico and Mexico.

—ISLAND LIVE OAK, *Q. tomentella* Engelm. is the species growing on the islands off the coast of Southern California. Acorn cups have tawny down.

Figure 163

8a Leaves deciduous 9

8b Leaves remaining on tree at least till spring 12

9a Leaves blue-green, not deeply lobed. Fig. 164. ....
.........................BLUE OAK, *Quercus douglasii* **Hook. & Arn.**

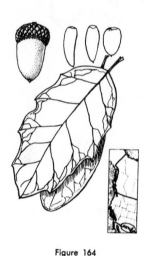

A tree with leaning or bent trunk, up to 40′ tall. The short, contorted, horizontal branches form a crown that is compact, flat and dome-like. The bark is a light, grayish brown. The blue-green leaves are variable in size and form, lighter below and covered with soft hairs. They are shed in autumn. The deep chestnut-brown acorns also vary greatly in size and shape. They mature in 1 season. The wood of this tree is used chiefly for fuel.

—MEXICAN BLUE OAK, *Quercus oblongifolia* Torr. has simple, entire, evergreen leaves. It extends up into Arizona, New Mexico and Texas.

Figure 164

9b Leaves deeply lobed 10

10a Leaves deep green, acorns slender. Fig. 165. ....
.................CALIFORNIA WHITE OAK, *Quercus lobata* **Nees**

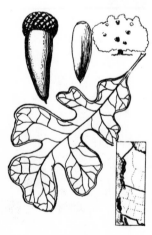

A massive tree, up to 80′ tall, with a short trunk, large, spreading branches and a dome-like crown. The bark is ashy gray to light brown and is broken up into rough, irregular blocks. The deep green leaves are leathery, covered with fine hair on both sides, lighter beneath and fall in the autumn. Male flowers are in hairy yellowish catkins, female are solitary and have broad stigmas. The long, slender acorns vary greatly in size, are plentiful and sweet. The Indians used to eat them, but now the farmers let their hogs fatten on them. The wood is dull brown, hard and brittle and is useful chiefly for fuel.

Figure 165

10b Found growing largely outside of California **11**

11a Acorns rounded, leaves deeply lobed. Fig. 166. ....
.................**OREGON WHITE OAK,** *Quercus garryana* **Dougl.**

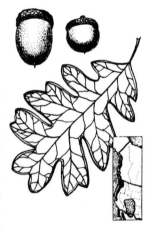

A tree up to 75′ tall with a short, clear trunk and broad round-topped crown. The bark is light, grayish brown with wide ridges and narrow, shallow furrows. The deep green, shiny leaves are thick and leathery, paler beneath and hairy. They are shed every fall. Male flowers are hairy catkins, female are sessile and solitary. The acorn is sweet, rounded, has a shallow cup and matures in one season. The wood is used for furniture and flooring as well as fuel.

—WAVYLEAF OAK, *Quercus undulata* Torr. This white oak is found throughout the Rocky Mountain area from Utah to Mexico and is characterized by wavy leaf margins.

Figure 166

—SANDPAPER OAK, *Q. pungens* Liebm. is found in East Texas, New Mexico and Arizona.

11b Leaf not as deeply lobed, acorns small, half covered by cup. Fig. 167. ....**GAMBEL OAK,** *Quercus gambelii* **Nutt.**

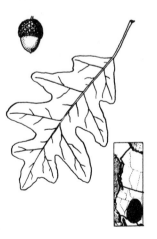

A small tree, up to 15′ tall, usually a shrub. The bark is grayish, rough and hard. The thin leaves are lobed moderately and the lobes are rounded. They are deciduous in the fall. The acorns are small and about half covered by the acorn cup. They mature in one season. This tree grows on the dry hillsides and because of its size it finds very little use except as ground cover.

—ORGAN MOUNTAINS OAK, *Q. organensis*, Trel. This rare oak is found only in the Organ Mountains of New Mexico.

—GRAY OAK, *Q. grisea* Liebm. occurs in West Texas, New Mexico and Arizona.

Figure 167

12a Leaves blue-green 13

12b Leaves shiny green, prickly, with rolled down margins 14

13a Acorns small and round, leaves spiny-toothed. Fig. 168. ....
...................**ARIZONA WHITE OAK,** *Quercus arizonica* **Sarg.**

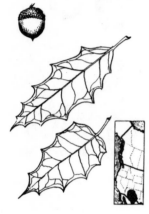

A smaller tree than the California White Oak, but it grows up to 60′ tall, has large branches and a more irregular crown. The bark is pale grayish, rough and broken up into hard ridges. The deep blue-green leaves are shiny above, leathery, lighter and slightly hairy beneath and remain on the tree throughout the winter. The acorns grow solitary or in pairs and mature in 1 season. It is used for fuel.

—JOLON OAK, *Q. jolonensis* Sarg. is found in Monterey County, California.

Figure 168

13b Acorns elongate, leaves vary from entire to toothed, yellowish underneath. Fig. 169. ....
..................**ENGELMANN OAK,** *Quercus engelmannii* **Greene**

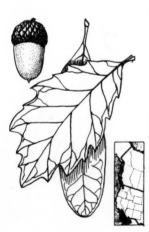

A short-trunked tree, up to 50′ tall, with horizontal branches and a dense, irregular, rounded crown. The pale grayish brown bark is deeply furrowed and widely ridged. Deep blue-green leaves are light yellow-green beneath and vary greatly in size and form. They may be entire or toothed and are evergreen. The acorns are dark, chestnut brown and have cups that are reddish brown and have sharp-pointed scales. They mature in one season. The wood is used for fuel in the desert country in which it grows. —NETLEAF OAK, *Q. reticulata* Humb. & Bonpl. This is an evergreen oak with blue-green leaves that show netted veins prominently. The acorns grow in long-stalked clusters. It occurs in Arizona, New Mexico and West Texas.

Figure 169

—SILVERLEAF OAK, *Q. hypoleucoides* A. Camus. This tree occurs in West Texas, New Mexico and Arizona. Its willow-like leaves are silvery white underneath.

14a Tree scrubby, leaves and acorns vary greatly. Fig. 170. ....
.................CALIFORNIA SCRUB OAK, *Quercus dumosa* **Nutt.**

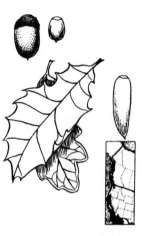

This tree grows up to 25' tall, usually scrubby and in dense thickets. The branches and twigs turn at abrupt angles and the light ashy gray bark is scaly and thin. Shiny green leaves are lighter and hairy beneath. Vary greatly in shape having irregular, spine-tipped teeth on the curled margins. They remain on the tree until spring. The acorns vary from short to long, but are usually slender. They mature in one season. The tree is useful for little more than ground cover.

—MACDONALD OAK, *Q. d. macdonaldi* Jeps. This variety is found on the islands off the coast of southern California.

—ALVORD OAK, *Q. d. alvordiana* Jeps. from the inner coast range of Southern California.

Figure 170

14b Trees larger, acorns slender and tapered. Fig. 171. ....
.................CALIFORNIA LIVE OAK, *Quercus agrifolia* **Nees**

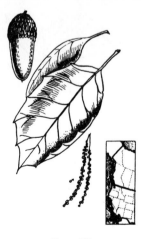

This short-trunked tree grows up to 75' tall and has long, crooked limbs. The dark bark has ashy white patches on the limbs. It is thick, hard and roughly furrowed on the lower portion. The holly-like leaves are dark, shiny green above, lighter and downy beneath, the edges curled down. They are stiff and brittle and remain on the tree until spring. The inconspicuous flowers appear in the spring. The acorns are slender, often pointed and mature in one season. The cups have scaly edges and turn in. The tree is used for tan bark and fuel. This tree is very common on the low hills and open valleys of most of California.

Figure 171

LEAVES SIMPLE, FRUIT BERRY-LIKE

1a Fruit a purple, waxy, berry-like nut. Fig. 172. ....
.....................PACIFIC BAYBERRY, *Myrica californica* Cham.

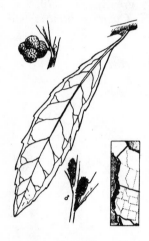

A small tree, up to 25' tall with a dense, narrow crown. The grayish brown bark is thin and smooth and shows reddish brown when cut. The leaves are evergreen, glossy, 2"-4 1/2" long, dark green above, paler beneath. They are often speckled with black, the edges are curled under and the blades are thin and tough. Male and female flowers are found on the same tree in short catkins, with the female above and male on the lower branches. The clusters of berry-like nuts are purplish but covered with a whitish, waxy bloom. Wax from the berries is used for commercial purposes. It was formerly known as Pacific Waxmyrtle.

Figure 172

1b Fruit other than above 2
2a Berry pendant from the mid-rib of a specialized leaf. Fig. 173.
............................AMERICAN BASSWOOD, *Tilia americana* L.

A large, spreading tree, up to 125' tall, with a light brown, deeply furrowed bark on a straight trunk. The dark green leaves are 5"-6" long, cordate and unequally lobed. Bees are very fond of the nectar from the yellowish-white flowers and for this reason these are often referred to as bee trees. The light, soft wood is useful for toys, wagon boxes and drawing boards.

—SMALLLEAF LINDEN, *Tilia cordata* Mill. This is a smaller tree wtih abundant flowers and fruit, but leaves only 1 1/2"-2 1/2" long.

Figure 173

2b Fruit other than above 3
3a Berries reddish when ripe 4
3b Berries not usually reddish 12

4a Blossom a large, white, 6-bract involucre. Fig. 174. ....
.....................PACIFIC DOGWOOD, *Cornus nuttallii* **Audubon**

A slender tree that grows to be up to 50' tall with a rounded crown, short trunk, and numerous small branches. The bark is thin and smooth with small reddish brown scales. The bright green leaves are shiny above, finely woolly beneath and 4"-5" long. The flowers are small, greenish yellow and in a compact head surrounded by 4-6 showy white bracts that are not notched as in the eastern dogwood. Bright red fruits, in clusters of 30-40 each contain 1 or 2 oblong, flattened seeds. This tree grows on moist well drained soil, usually in the shade. It is an ornamental tree and the flowers are protected by law in most of its range.

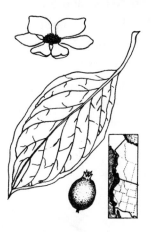

Figure 174

4b Not as above 5

5a Berries in drooping clusters, bark brownish red, peels in scales.
Fig. 175. ....PACIFIC MADRONE, *Arbutus menziesii* **Pursh**

A colorful tree, up to 80' tall, with a leaning trunk, heavy branches and a rounded crown. The red-brown bark is thin and smooth and is shed in large scales somewhat like Sycamore bark. The dark green leaves are thick, leathery, smooth, shiny above and whitish below, 2 1/2"-5" long and remain on the tree till the new ones form. The white flowers in large loose panicles mature into clusters of orange-red berries that are nearly 1/2" in diameter. Wood of the tree is used for cabinet work and charcoal.

—ARIZONA MADRONE, *A, arizonica* Sarg. In this tree the bark is dark red on twigs, but ashy gray on the trunk. The leaves are narrower and the trunk usually straighter. Grows in S. W. New Mexico and Southern Arizona.

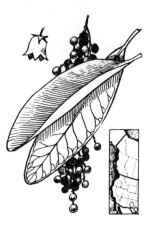

Figure 175

—TEXAS MADRONE, *A. texana* Buckl. is found in S. E. New Mexico and S. W. Texas.

5b Not as above **6**

6a Berries in upright clusters. SUMACS ....**page 140**

6b Berries not as above **7**

7a Leaves with spiny points on the margins **8**

7b Leaves not spiny **9**

8a Leaves with long barbs. Fig. 176. ....
...................................**AMERICAN HOLLY,** *Ilex opaca* **Ait.**

A tree up to 80′ tall with light gray bark and sharp-pointed, evergreen leaves. This tree is planted for its leaves and berries that are used for Christmas decorations. It is a native of the eastern states.

Figure 176

8b Leaves with sharp-toothed margins, berries red, larger at the flower end. Fig. 177. ....
......................**CHRISTMASBERRY,** *Photinia arbutifolia* **Lindl.**

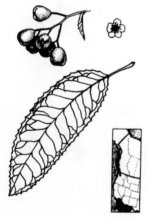

A shrub to tree up to 25′ tall with a short, thick trunk and many upright branches. The smooth, pale gray bark is indistinctly seamed. Leaves are thick, leathery, smooth, shiny, deep green above and paler beneath, evergreen. Small white flowers form clusters 2″-3″ in diameter. The bright red berries are borne in large clusters. They are larger at the flower end and indistinctly 3-lobed.

Figure 177

9a Berries large, 1"-3" in diameter 10

9b Berries small, less than 1" diameter 11

10a Berries tomato-shaped, seeds flattened. Fig. 178. ....
.................COMMON PERSIMMON, *Diospyros virginiana* L.

A tree up to 50' tall with bark that
is nearly black. Has dark green, shiny
leaves, 4"-6" long and creamy, bell-
shaped flowers. The edible fruit is
tomato-shaped, 1"-2" in diameter and
is usually picked after the first frost.
The tree is cultivated for its fruit in
the southern states. This odd tasting
fruit is greatly relished by some and
equally despised by others.

Figure 178

10b Berries large, compartments inside filled with seeds. Fig. 179.
....POMEGRANATE, *Punica granatum* L.

A small bushy tree, up to 15' tall,
with large, shiny, green leaves and
showy white flowers. The wrinkled
fruits are brownish red, 2"-3" in diameter and have a persistent calyx. The
edible portion of the fruit is the wine-
colored pulp between the numerous
seeds. Several varieties with showy blossoms are grown in the southwest for
their ornamental value only.

Figure 179

11a Leaves silvery white, heavy and leathery. Fig. 180. ....
........SILVERY BUFFALOBERRY, *Shepherdia argentea* Nutt.

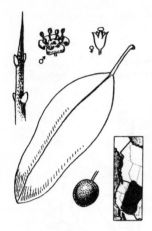

A shrubby tree up to 20′ tall with smooth, light, grayish green bark and thorny twigs. The leaves are heavy and leathery, silvery above and downy beneath. The 4-petaled flowers have exserted stamens and recurved petals on the male. The female are smaller, bell-shaped and on different trees. The fruit is a bright red, tart, but edible berry. This tree grows in the more open country of the plains.

Figure 180

11b Leaves deep green, netted and pointed. Fig. 181. ....
.....................NETLEAF HACKBERRY, *Celtis reticulata* Torr.

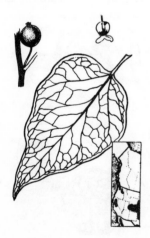

A short-trunked tree that grows up to 30′ tall and has a rounded crown. The ashy gray bark is rough and has numerous, thin projecting ridges. The leaves are thick, leathery, deep green above and pale yellow-green and rough beneath. The veins are usually prominent and the edges entire. Male flowers are clustered, female are solitary, green and have a cleft stigma. The fruit is a small red-orange berry. The tree is useful for fuel and ground cover and is sometimes planted as an ornamental.

12a Berries yellow-green, olive-like, leaves aromatic. Fig. 182. ......
.........CALIFORNIA-LAUREL, *Umbellularia californica* **Nutt.**

A tree up to 80′ tall with a straight, heavy trunk and a wide spreading, dense, rounded crown. The dark, reddish brown bark is thin, and scaly, smoother on the branches. The deep yellow-green leaves are shiny, 3″-6″ long and remain on the tree 2 years. They have a strong aroma of camphor. The small flowers are fragrant and bloom in midwinter. Yellow-green fruits similar to olives contain 1 large, thin-shelled seed. The wood of this tree has an exceptionally beautiful grain and is highly prized for manufacturing veneer and novelties. It is usually sold as Oregon Myrtle.

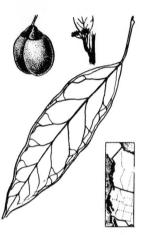

Figure 182

12b Berries blue to black when ripe **13**

13a Berries 3-lobed, containing 3 nutlets, blossoms blue. CEA-NOTHUS **14**

13b Berries containing 1-3 seeds **16**

14a Twigs spiny, leaves not prominently 3-veined, margins entire. Fig. 183. ......SPINY CEANOTHUS, *Ceanothus spinosus* **Nutt.**

A small tree, usually a shrub, up to 15′ tall, with a short, clear trunk and a narrow open crown. The bark is deep reddish brown and scaly. The leaves are thick, leathery, smooth, 3/4″-1″ long, partly evergreen, usually entire, sometimes serrate at the tip. The blue flowers grow in large fragrant panicles. Three thin-shelled nuts join together on one stem and each contains a seed. These nuts are smooth and black when ripe. This tree grows in the light gravelly soil of rocky canyons.

Figure 183

14b Leaves prominently 3-veined **15**

15a Leaves with dense hair on the under side. Fig. 184. ....
........FELTLEAF CEANOTHUS, *Ceanothus arboreus* Greene

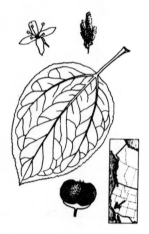

A low, short-trunked tree, usually bushy, up to 20' tall. The bark is deep brown and has thick, square scales. The deep green leaves are thick, densely hairy beneath and have hairy stems. Pale blue flowers form large dense panicles. The 3-lobed fruit is black and has wrinkled nutlets. The tree has no commercial use but serves as ground cover and is attractive in bloom.

Figure 184

15b Leaves only slightly hairy and narrower than above. Fig. 185.
....................BLUEBLOSSOM, *Ceanothus thyrsiflorus* Eschsch.

A thick, short, bushy tree up to 25' tall, usually a shrub. The twigs are angular in cross section and the clear reddish brown bark has thin scales. The leaves are evergreen, smooth, shiny and lighter beneath. Light blue flowers are small but form large dense clusters. The 3-lobed fruit is black and has smooth nutlets.

There are many more forms of ceanothus, or myrtles as they are usually called, but most of them are shrub forms. They are valuable as ground cover to slow down the runoff of heavy rains and prevent hillsides from washing away. They also form an important browse for range cattle and deer.

Figure 185

16a Fruit cherry-like but with 2-3 pits 17

16b Fruit not cherry-like **18**

17a Leaf finely serrate. Fig. 186. ....…..............................
.................CASCARA BUCKTHORN, *Rhamnus purshiana* **DC.**

A slender tree up to 40′ tall with light gray, smooth outer bark. The glossy, dark green leaves, 4″-6″ long are minutely toothed. Small greenish flowers borne in the leaf axils mature into bitter black berries with 2-3 seeds in them that are relished by bears and pigeons. The strongly laxative bark is collected for medicinal use.

Figure 186

17b Leaf margins sharply toothed. Fig. 187. ....
........HOLLYLEAF BUCKTHORN, *Rhamnus crocea ilicifolia*
Greene

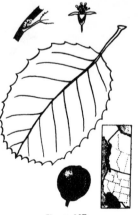

A shrub or slender tree up to 15′ tall with smooth, dull, ashy gray bark. The shiny, yellow-green leaves are thin and leathery, margins are prickly, evergreen. Flowers are inconspicuous in small clusters in leaf axils. Dull red berries contain 1-3 nuts.

—GREAT REDBERRY BUCKTHORN, *R. c. pirifolia* Little is found on the Santa Rosa, Santa Cruz, Santa Catalina, San Clemente and Guadalupe Islands.

Figure 187

18a Twigs not thorny **20**

18b Twigs with long thorns **19**

19a **Leaves broad, doubly serrate at the tip end. Fig. 188.** ....
..................**BLACK HAWTHORN,** *Crataegus douglasii* **Lindl.**

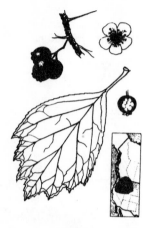

This shrubby tree may grow up to 30' tall, but is generally found in dense, impenetrable thickets. The finely seamed bark is reddish gray on the trunk to red on the twigs. Deep green leaves are thick, leathery and smooth above. The white, showy flowers have 5 petals that are not nearly as long as they are on the Service-berries. The berries are shiny, purple to black when ripe. They are edible, but tasteless. The birds eat them in winter and spring.

—WILLIAMS HAWTHORN, *C. williamsii* Eggl. This species is found in Montana.

Figure 188

19b **Leaves narrower, finely serrate, may be toothed. Fig. 189.**
................**WILLOW HAWTHORN,** *Crataegus saligna* **Greene**

A small tree, up to 20' tall, with long, flexible branches. The bark is scaly, grayish and thin. Long, slender, black thorns are found on the twigs. The leaves are small, 1/2"-3/4" long, and have the appearance of willow leaves. White 5-petaled flowers are found in clusters near the branch ends. The berries are almost black and round with a conspicuous calyx. This tree grows in the canyons of Central Colorado up to an altitude of 7000'.

—ENGLISH HAWTHORN, *Crataegus oxyacantha L.* A small tree, up to 20' tall with a rough, scaly bark and thorny twigs. The shiny, green leaves are broad, lobed and sometimes compound. Flowers may be single or double and range from scarlet to white in the many varieties. The berries are red and have 2 seeds in them.

Figure 189

20a Berries with distinct calyx at the end. Fig. 190. ....
.........**PACIFIC SERVICEBERRY,** *Amelanchier florida* **Lindl.**

A small slender tree up to 15′ tall with
smooth, dark, ashy gray bark. The leaves
are dark green, smooth above, 2 1/2″-4″
long and serrated at the tip end. Showy
white blossoms form loose, pendant racemes. The flowers have 5 long petals.
Berries turn dark purple to black in mid-
summer. They are about 1/4″ or more
in diameter, have a conspicuous calyx,
are edible and often delicious. The trees
form dense thickets on large areas of
mountainside. The wood was used by
the Indians for bows and the berries
were eaten raw or compounded into a
pemmican mixture with meat.

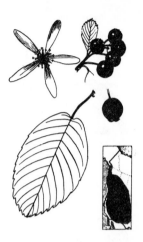

—UTAH SERVICEBERRY, A. *utahensis*
Koehne. This species is more common
east of the Rockies. The tree is larger,
leaves sparsely hairy beneath.

Figure 190

20b Flowers and fruit grow on long tassels. Fig. 191. ....
...............**WAVYLEAF SILKTASSEL,** *Garrya elliptica* **Dougl.**

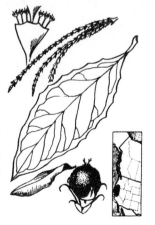

A shrub or small tree, up to 30′ tall,
with a short trunk and bitter bark. Evergreen leaves are thick, leathery, opposite, smooth above, woolly beneath and
have wavy margins. Male and female
flowers grow on different trees. The
male flowers grow on elongate tassels,
3″-5″ long. The purplish berry-like fruits
grow in clusters, have a strongly acid
pulp and contain 1-2 seeds each. The
wood is hard and heavy, but the tree
forms are so rare that it finds no commercial use.

Figure 191

FRUIT WITH SINGLE PIT

1a Fruits containing solid pits 2

1b Fruits containing seed in a 2-part woody shell 4

2a Fruit 3″-5″ long. Fig. 192. AVOCADO, *Persea americana* Mill.

A medium sized tree, up to 60′ tall with many branches and large, 4″-10″ long, shiny leaves that are bright green. The fruit is pear-shaped to ovoid, green, fleshy and contains a large pit. Native to Central America but cultivated commercially in southern California. The light greenish flesh is buttery and can easily be spread on bread.

Figure 192

2b Fruit much smaller 3

3a Fruit 1/2″-1 1/2″ long, dark green to black. Fig. 193. ....
....COMMON OLIVE, *Olea europaea* L.

A rounded orchard tree up to 30′ tall and with smooth gray bark. The leaves are opposite, evergreen, leathery, dull green above, silvery beneath. The fruit is the common olive sold in stores. It is a native of the Eastern Mediterranean area but cultivated in Central California for its fruit. The olives are canned ripe or green and stuffed. Olive oil is also expressed from the fruit and sold.

Figure 193

3b Fruit 1/2″ long, silvery, leaves also silvery. Fig. 194. ....
...................................**RUSSIAN-OLIVE,** *Eleagnus angustifolia* **L.**

A small tree or shrub up to 20′ tall with smooth bark and white branchlets. Leaves are deciduous, light green above, silvery beneath. Tubular flowers, yellow, in leaf axils. Fruit silvery, olive shaped. An ornamental tree not related to the olive family as the hyphenated common name indicates. Planted for its limited size and silvery leaves.

—CAMPHOR-TREE, *Cinnamomum camphora* Nees & Eberm. This evergreen tree has light green leaves that give off a strong aroma when crushed. Its fruit is a small berry with one seed. A native of southern China it is planted as an ornamental in the southern states.

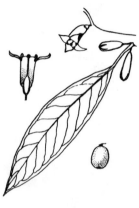

Figure 194

4a Pit roughened and horny, fruit covered with fine hair. Fig. 195.
....**PEACH,** *Prunus persica* Batsch.

A small tree, up to 25′ tall, with dark, finely ribbed bark. Long narrow leaves are bright green, petioles often red. Blossoms pink to red-violet. Fruit smooth but covered with a velvety down, median groove prominent. Originally from China but cultivated from southern British Columbia south to California. Many commercial varieties have been developed.

Ornamental varieties with more numerous and more deeply colored blossoms, but smaller fruit have also been developed and are commonly planted.

Figure 195

4b Pits smooth, fruit not downy **5**

5a Blossoms pink to white, fruit with deep median groove. Fig. 196.
....APRICOT, *Prunus armeniaca* L.

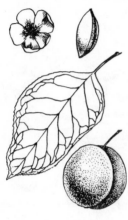

A small, rounded tree up to 20′ tall, with reddish brown bark. The rounded leaves are dark green and shiny above, hairy beneath. Blossoms come out before the leaves and are pink to white. The fruit is yellow-orange, round, has deep median groove and is very finely hairy. The pit is smooth and the seed almond-shaped. Native of China but grown in the same area as the peach.
—ALMOND, *P. amygdalus Batsch.* is a tree similar to the two above, but it is grown for its pit which is the almond nut, while the fleshy husk is discarded. It is grown commercially in California.

Figure 196

5b Fruit not as above 6

6a Pit elongate, PLUMS 7

6b Pit rounded, CHERRIES 9

7a Fruit dark purple when ripe. Fig. 197. ....
....GARDEN PLUM, *Prunus domestica* L.

A small tree up to 15′ tall with pale gray, smooth bark and spreading branches. The leaves are medium green and the blossoms white. The fruit is dark, bluish purple with a whitish bloom. This description is that of the common prune. There are many other varieties of this species such as the following:
—PEACH PLUM, peach shaped and rosy.
—EGG PLUM, yellow or purplish, egg size and shape.
—GREENGAGE, yellow-green, small and rounded.
—PETITE PLUM, reddish purple and still smaller, round.

Figure 197

7b Fruit smaller than above, grows wild 8

8a Fruit yellow to orange, leaf elliptic, found west of Rockies.
   Fig. 198. ....KLAMATH PLUM, *Prunus subcordata* Benth.

A short-trunked tree up to 20' tall, with heavy branches that grow at right angles to the trunk. Twigs are spiny. The bark is ashy brown, seamed and scaly on the lower part. The leaves are dark green and shiny above, lighter and hairy beneath, 1 1/4"-3" long, round to elliptic in shape. White blossoms appear before the leaves in the spring. They are about 1/2" in diameter. The plum is 3/4"-1" long, egg-shaped, purple-red to yellow when it ripens in late August. The fruit is edible but usually this species does not bear as well as the American.

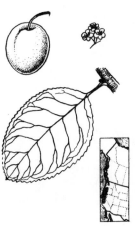

Figure 198

8b Fruit more reddish, leaf pointed, found east of the Rockies.
   Fig. 199. ....AMERICAN PLUM, *Prunus americana* Marsh.

This tree is also small, up to 20' tall, with branches similar to the above. The bark is ashy gray and fairly thick. Dark green leaves, 2 1/2"-4" long, are paler beneath and show strongly reticulated veins. They are pointed and sharply serrate. The showy white flowers, 3/4" in diameter, mature into red to orange plums that are about 3/4" in diameter. The skin is leathery, but the flesh is usually sweet, though the taste varies from tree to tree. Both edges are sharp on the pit. The fruit is used for food and the roots are used for grafting stock.

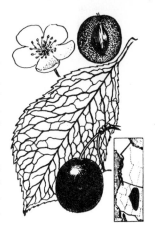

Figure 199

9a Cherries borne in clusters 10

9b Cherries borne in a raceme 12

10a Cherries bright red, small, 1/4″ in diameter. Fig. 200. ....
....**PIN CHERRY**, *Prunus pensylvanica* L.

Figure 200

A tree up to 40′ tall with a slender trunk and slender, upright branches. The bark is smooth, wine colored and thin. The lenticels show up strongly and stretch into horizontal lines on older trunks. Shining green leaves are acuminate and have long-pointed tips. White blossoms in clusters of 4-5 decorate the tree in early May. The cherries are about 1/4″ in diameter, red, acid but sweet and juicy. They make good jelly and are equally good when eaten raw.

10b Cherries larger 11

11a Cherries yellow to reddish, tart. Fig. 201. ....
....**SOUR CHERRY**, *Prunus cerasus* L.

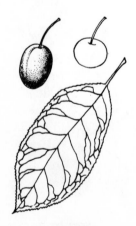

Figure 201

A small tree up to 30′ tall with wide-spreading, drooping branchlets. The bark is smooth, pale reddish gray. Bright green leaves are smooth. Cherries are yellow to reddish, tart, 1/2″-3/4″ in diameter. Blossoms white. This tree is a native of Europe. Planted as an ornamental tree and also in orchards as a pie cherry.

11b Cherries dark red, sweet. Fig. 202. ....
....MAZZARD CHERRY, *Prunus avium* **L.**

A large orchard tree up to 75′ tall with bark reddish brown, peels horizontally like the birches. The dark green leaves are 4″-6″ long. White blossoms appear at the same time as the leaves. There are many varieties and the fruit may be deep red to yellow. This is the common sweet cherry, a native of Europe but grown as far north as the Okanagan in British Columbia and throughout the western states.

Figure 202

12a Cherries black, on a long raceme. Fig. 203. ....
......WESTERN CHOKECHERRY, *Prunus virginiana demissa*
Torr.

A small tree up to 18′ tall with a smooth, deep brown bark that becomes rough in age. The dark green leaves are smooth above, 2″-4″ long, acuminate. The abundant white flowers grow on pendant racemes. The pea-sized cherries are dark red to black when ripe and are very astringent. Consumed by humans but mostly by bears.

—BLACK CHOKECHERRY, *P. v. melanocarpa* Sarg. This variety growing just east of the Rockies has thicker leaves and darker berries.

—SOUTHWESTERN BLACK CHERRY, *P. serotina rufula* McVaugh is a species found in Arizona and New Mexico. It is characterized by petioles without glands.

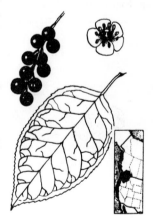

Figure 203

—CATALINA CHERRY, *P. lyonii* Sarg. On this tree, growing on Catalina Island, the cherries are very large, 1″ in diameter and the leaves are thick, leathery, entire, ovate, and evergreen.

—HOLLYLEAF CHERRY, *P. ilicifolia* Dietr. This is a closely allied tree, also evergreen. It has thick, leathery leaves that are spine-toothed. It grows on the southern California coast.

12b Cherries dark red, on a short, loose raceme. Fig. 204. ....
......................BITTER CHERRY, *Prunus emarginata* D. Dietr.

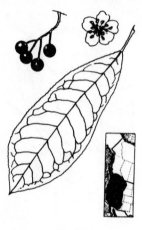

A small tree up to 40′ tall with thin grayish brown bark that is smooth and reddish on the twigs. The elliptical to oblanceolate leaves are about 2″ long, finely serrated and have a bitter almond odor. The white flowers are fragrant and have emarginate calyx lobes. Cherries are dark red when ripe and are quite bitter. The inner bark was used by the Indians to fasten feathers to the arrows used in aquatic hunting since it would not stretch when wet.

Figure 204

1a Fruit an apple 2

1b Fruit not an apple 3

2a Fruit large, 2″-4″ diameter. Fig. 205. ....
......................................DOMESTIC APPLE, *Malus pumila* Mill.

FRUIT A POME, APPLE TYPE

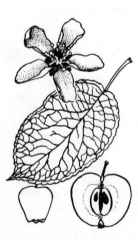

An orchard tree up to 30′ tall with spreading branches and a grayish brown bark that flakes off in curls. The leaves are shiny, medium green and the blossoms are white to pink. The fruit is a fleshy pome with a 5-chambered core containing numerous dark brown seeds. There are many varieties of apples and they range in color from green and yellow to black-red. In shape they may be round, depressed at both ends or elongate with 5 points at the flower end. There are also several varieties of crab apples in cultivation. They are smaller, more tart and have a proportionately longer stem. The trees are usually taller and have a narrower crown than apple trees.

Figure 205

2b Fruit much smaller, oblong. Fig. 206. ....
.....................OREGON CRAB APPLE, *Malus diversifolia* **Roem.**

A small tree, up to 30' tall, it has an irregular crown and grows in dense, spiny thickets. The bark is smooth and light brown in young trees, but as they become older it changes to dark brown and is rough and scaly. The leaves are dark green above, paler and hairy beneath, 2"-4" long and have serrate edges that are often also toothed or lobed. The 5-petaled blossoms are white and fragrant. Fruit is oblong 1/2"-3/4" long, dull yellow when ripe and extremely sour. Where it is plentiful the fruit is sometimes used for jellies and preserves. The rootstocks are used as grafting stock for commercial varieties of apple trees.

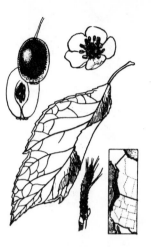

Figure 206

3a Fruit pear-shaped, smooth. Fig. 207. ....
....DOMESTIC PEAR, *Pyrus communis* **L.**

Pear trees are taller than apple trees, up to 60' tall, and have more erect branches. The gray bark is broken into squared plates on the trunk. The leaves are dark green, shiny and smooth. White blossoms mature into fruit that is yellow-green when ripe and may be almost round to pear-shaped. Pears have been introduced from Europe and several varieties are commercially cultivated in the West.

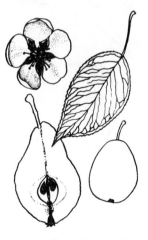

Figure 207

3b Fruit pear-shaped, not smooth but hairy. Fig. 208. ....
....QUINCE, *Cydonia oblonga* Mill.

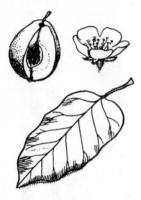

A small tree, up to 20′ tall with a rounded top, crooked branches and dark gray bark. The dull green leaves are hairy beneath, 2″-4″ long. Large, showy blossoms, 1″-2″ in diameter, are white to pink and mature into a pear-shaped, fragrant fruit that is covered with fine hair and turns from green to yellow when ripe. It is a native of Asia and is cultivated occasionally in the West for its fruit and flowers.

Figure 208

FRUIT A CITROCARP.

1a Fruit yellow to orange, flesh divided into radical sections. Fig. 209. ....SWEET ORANGE, *Citrus sinensis* Osbeck

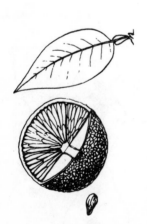

A small orchard tree, up to 15′ tall with dark gray bark and a dense rounded crown. The blossoms are white and the dark green leaves are evergreen. The fruit matures in the winter. In the citrus genus there are several species and many varieties cultivated in California and Arizona. The most common ones are listed below:

—LEMON. Oblong-shaped, yellow, tart, cultivated commercially in California and Arizona.

—GRAPEFRUIT. Twice as large as oranges, round, yellow, tart but sweet, flesh yellowish or pink.

Figure 209

—TANGERINE ORANGE. A small orange that is sweet and peels easily.

—LIME. A greenish, lemon-shaped fruit that is tart and odd flavored.

1b Fruit similar but wrinkled, sections filled with seeds. POME-
GRANATE ....page 93

FRUIT AN AGGREGATE OR MULTIPLE.

1a Fruit a hard, green, orange-sized ball. Fig. 210. ....
...................................OSAGE-ORANGE, *Maclura pomifera* Sch.

A tree up to 60′ tall with orange colored roots and stout thorns on the
branches. The orange-brown bark peels
in longitudinal strips. The bright green,
smooth leaves are deciduous. Male and
female flowers grow on different trees.
The fruit is a dense green ball, 2″ in
diameter composed of numerous seeds.
It turns yellow when ripe and exudes a
milky sap when cut. A native of the central states it is used for windbreaks and
fence lines in the west.

Figure 210

1b Fruit not as above 2

2a Fruit a fleshy bag containing numerous small seeds. Fig. 211.
....COMMON FIG, *Ficus carica* L.

A tree up to 30′ tall with smooth, purplish gray bark and deciduous leaves
4″-8″ long. The flowers are axillary inside a fleshy receptacle that matures
into the greenish to purple fruit. Figs
are native to the Mediterranean region
and are grown commercially in California. The black Mission Figs were introduced into California by the early Span-
ish priests.
—INDIA RUBBER TREE, *F. elastica*
Roxbg. This tree with the broad, shiny
leaves is popular in Southern California
parks and is also often grown as a potted
plant.

Figure 211

2b Fruit a berry-like aggregate. Fig. 212. ....
....RED MULBERRY, *Morus rubra* L.

A tree up to 70' tall with light brown bark and milky sap. The leaves are prominently veined blue-green and may vary from entire to lobed. Male flowers are axillary spikes, female are urn-shaped. Fruits are in the form of a seed surrounded by fleshy, edible lobes. It has escaped from cultivation in parts of the west.

—BLACK MULBERRY, *M. nigra* L. This tree has berries that are dark red to black and leaves that are not as often lobed. It is a native of Western Asia.

—WHITE MULBERRY, *M. alba* L. This native of China has white berries and leaves that are smooth above.

Figure 212

FRUIT A HOP-LIKE CONE

1a Seeds large, shiny, black. Leaves entire, shiny, heavy. Fig. 213.
............................SOUTHERN MAGNOLIA, *Magnolia grandiflora* L.

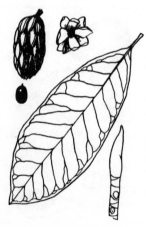

A tree up to 100' tall with a gray to light brown bark covered with small, flat scales. The shiny, bright green leaves are rusty beneath and have prominent veins. Large flowers, 7"-8" across, have 9-12 petals and are bright violet in the center. The fruit is a hop-like arrangement with a black seed in each of the many cells. Native of the southern states it does well in damp, rich soil and moderate climates along the west coast.

Figure 213'

1b Fruit a tapered upright cone, seeds small, leaves 4-pointed. Fig. 214. ....YELLOW-POPLAR, *Liriodendron tulipifera* **L.**

This large, beautiful tree, up to 200' tall with deeply furrowed bark has been introduced from the eastern states. It can easily be identified by its peculiarly 4-pointed, dark green leaves. The large flowers, 1 1/2"-2" long, are tulip-like with 6 pale green petals that are orange striped in the throat. Fruits are dry and cone-like. It is cultivated as a park and lawn tree. Often called Tuliptree for its flowers.

Figure 214

FRUIT A CAPSULE CONTAINING SEEDS

1a Fruiting head ball-like 2
1b Fruit not as above 5
2a Leaf entire, head contains small cone-shaped pods. Fig. 215. ....COMMON BUTTONBUSH, *Cephalanthus occidentalis* **L.**

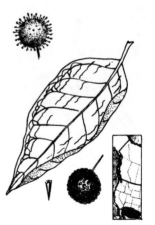

A shrub or a tree sometimes as tall as 30', with a blackish brown bark that is rough and deeply furrowed with wide ridges. The yellow-green leaves are smooth above, lighter below and hairy, 3"-6" long, opposite or whorled. The cream-colored flowers are fragrant and in dense, ball-like heads. The fruiting head contains numerous cone-shaped pods each with 1-4 seeds. It is useful chiefly as ground cover.

Figure 215

2b Other than as above 3
3a Leaf star-shaped 4

3b Leaf broad, maple-like, bark deciduous. Fig. 216. ....
................LONDON PLANETREE, *Platanus acerifolia* **Willd.**

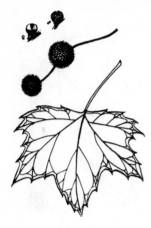

A tree up to 70′ tall with pale greenish gray to cream-colored bark. Large scales peeling off the limbs and bark give it a patchy appearance. The leaves are 4″-6″ across and are yellow-green. Male and female flowers are both ball-shaped and occur on the same tree. The fruit is a brownish ball, 1″ in diameter, composed of numerous seeds. There are usually 2 balls on a stem 3″-6″ long. This popular shade tree is said to be a cross between the Oriental Plane and the American Sycamore.

Figure 216

4a Fruit 2-3 on a stem, park peels in large flakes. Fig. 217. ....
................CALIFORNIA SYCAMORE, *Platanus racemosa* **Nutt.**

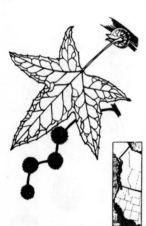

A short-trunked tree up to 75′ tall with large, heavy branches that are likely to go in almost any direction. At the base the bark is dull brown, ridged and furrowed, but on the rest of the tree it is smooth, ashy white, with grayish green areas where flakes have peeled off. The leaves are light yellow-green, paler beneath, 5″-11″ wide and densely hairy beneath. Male and female flowers form heads on a thread-like stem. The fruiting heads are about 1″ in diameter, 4-5 on one stem that may be 5″-10″ long. These trees grow on poor rocky soil along river beds and the course of streams.

Figure 217

—ARIZONA SYCAMORE, *P. wrightii* S. Wats. On this more eastern tree the leaves are more deeply lobed, with entire edges and the fruiting heads are usually found only 2-3 on one stem. Grows in New Mexico, Arizona, and Southern California.

4b Fruit in single heads on one stem, bark furrowed. Fig. 218. ....
...................................SWEETGUM, *Liquidambar styraciflua* **L.**

A tree up to 140' tall with dark, reddish brown bark that is furrowed and scaly. The star-shaped leaves are 5-lobed, bright green, 5"-7" long and turn crimson before they fall. The fruits are dry balls, 1 1/2" in diameter, composed of 2-horned capsules. It is a native of the eastern states, planted as an ornamental and park tree in the west.

Figure 218

5a Capsule beaked **16**

5b Fruit not a beaked capsule **6**

6a Fruit in a long pencil-sized pod **7**

6b Fruit capsule not as above **8**

7a Leaf linear, seeds tufted. Fig. 219. ....
.............................DESERTWILLOW, *Chilopsis linearis* **Sweet.**

A small tree, up to 20' tall, with slim upright branches and a crooked, often leaning trunk. The blackish bark is narrowly seamed with hard, connected ridges. The leaves are smooth, 5"-6" long, linear to linear lanceolate, willow-like, pale gray to yellow-green. They remain on the tree till mid-winter. The large white flowers are catalpa-like, have purple and yellow markings in the throat and give off the odor of violets. Fruit pods are slim, round, 5"-10" long and straw-colored. The seeds are double, flattened, small with a fringe of down at each end. Ranchers prize the hard, durable wood for fence posts.

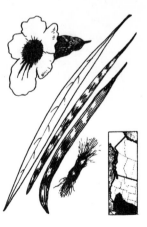

Figure 219

7b Leaf large, heart-shaped, pod 8″-20″ long. Fig. 220. ....
.....................NORTHERN CATALPA, *Catalpa speciosa* **Warder**

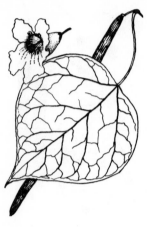

A spreading tree, up to 120′ tall with thick, furrowed, brown bark and heavy limbs. The heart-shaped leaves are light green, hairy beneath, 7″-15″ long and turn black before they fall. Large, white, showy flowers in erect clusters are faintly spotted with brown. It can be immediately identified as a catalpa by the cylindrical pencil pod 8″-20″ long. Native of the central states it is often planted for its showy blossoms and large leaves.

—COMMON CATALPA, *C. bignonioides* Walt. has white flowers spotted with yellow and purple in the throats.

Figure 220

8a Leaf heart-shaped, large, 1″ capsule rounded, 2-celled. Fig. 221.
......ROYAL PAULOWNIA, *Paulownia tomentosa* **Sieb. & Zucc.**

A tree that grows up to 40′ tall and has dark gray furrowed bark. The leaves are large, 7″-14″ long, light green and hairy on both sides. The purplish flowers, 2″ long, hang in loose panicles. The fruit is a round, woody, 2-celled capsule 1″-1 1/2″ in diameter. A native of China this tree is widely planted in parks and gardens.

Figure 221

8b Capsule less than half the size of the above 9

9a Capsules 5-valved, leaf linear. Fig. 222. ....
........TORREY VAUQUELINIA, *Vauquelinia californica* Sarg.

A small tree, up to 20′ tall with an up-right trunk and crooked branches. The bark is dark, reddish brown and scaly. The bright yellow-green leaves are smooth above and woolly beneath and have a heavy mid-rib. The 5-petaled flowers are 1/4″ in diameter, bright red, but form hoary panicles. The pointed capsules are 1/4″ long and remain on the tree until spring when the 5 sides open and shed the seed. This tree is of no commercial use and is found in the rocky gullies and bottoms of the south-west.

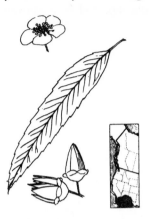

Figure 222

9b Capsules not 5-valved 10

10a Capsules 2-valved, small 11

10b Capsules not 2-valved 12

11a Smooth, black capsules contain 1 black seed, leaves spatulate. Fig. 223. ....GUM BUMELIA, *Bumelia lanuginosa* Pers.

A straight-trunked tree, up to 50′ tall with a round-topped crown and spiny branches. The dark grayish brown bark has thick scales that form ridges. Leaves are shiny, dark green above and rusty or silvery white beneath. Small ovoid flow-ers grow in axillary clusters. Each flower produces a small oval capsule. When the two halves open up a black seed about half as large as the capsule drops out. This tree is found in the canyons and mountains of the southwest. It produces large quantities of clear viscous gum.

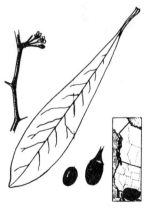

Figure 223

11b Capsules containing more than one seed 17

12a 4-parted fruit capsule turns scarlet when ripe. Fig. 224. ....
...................WESTERN WAHOO, *Euonymus occidentalis* **Nutt.**

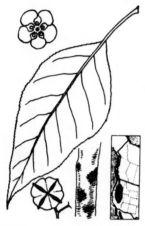

A small, slender tree with ashy gray-ish, ridged bark. The leaves are ovate, pointed, with finely serrate edges, dark green turning to bright yellow in fall. Purple, 4-5 petaled flowers grow in axillary clusters and mature into 4-lobed, pale violet fruits, 1/2" across that turn scarlet when ripe. The tree is rare and has no commercial use.

Figure 224

12b Capsules not 4-parted 13

13a Capsules clustered around twigs. Fig. 225. ....
.............PINK MELALEUCA, *Melaleuca nesophila* **F. Muell.**

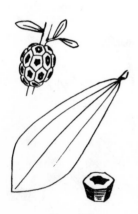

A small, slender tree up to 30' tall with spongy bark. The rose-colored flowers are clustered about the stem. Seed capsules later replace them in closely packed groups. There are a large number of different species of Melaleuca imported from Australia and grown in the southwest. Their leaf forms vary from needles to broadleafs, but the seed clusters are characteristic of all.

—LEMON BOTTLEBRUSH, *Callistemon lanceolatus* DC. This is the most commonly planted species of the Callistemon genus. It has bright red flowers in clusters 2"-4" long. The long-stamened flowers encircling stem resemble a bottlebrush and give the genus its name.

Figure 225

13b Capsules not clustered around the stem 14
14a capsule cup-shaped, bark shredding. Fig. 226. ....
.....................................**BLUE GUM,** *Eucalyptus globulus* **Labill.**

A gigantic tree, over 200' tall in this country and quite a lot taller in Australia from where it has been introduced. The aromatic bark is rough and ragged and peels off in long strips. Leaves are ever-green, leathery, pale green and turn their edges to the sun. The fruit and flower are in a cone-shaped capsule. Many other gum trees are also planted in the southwest. The wood is useful for fuel and stands up well as piles in salt water.

Figure 226

—RED GUM, *E. rostrata* Schlecht, (Fig. 227) is slower growing, hardier, has fruit capsules 1/4" in diameter with a 4-beaked top, and leaves 4"-6" long. Its wood is more durable than that of the Blue Gum.

—SUGAR GUM, *E. corynocalyx* F. v.M. This is a smaller tree with long, narrow leaves 3"-6" long. Fruit capsules are barrel-shaped, 1/2" long, short-stalked, 5-10 in a cluster. It is drought resistant and makes good firewood.

—SCARLET GUM, *E. ficifolia* F. v.M. A small tree, up to 35' tall, with wider leaves and flowers that are pink to scarlet. It is also drought resistant and is planted as a shade tree along streets.

—REDBOX, *E. polyanthemos* Schau. A medium-sized gum tree with broad, gray-green leaves and large clusters of small white flowers. It resists frost and drought, attracts bees and is often planted as a windbreak.

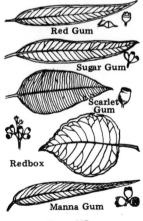

—MANNA GUM, *E. viminalis* Labill. A tall tree with drooping branchlets and bark that is usually persistent. Leaves are green on both sides, long, and narrow. Capsules are spherical, about 1/4" long. A fast growing species commonly planted for shade.

Figure 227

14b Capsule not cup-like **15**

15a Fruit a several-celled capsule, tree very thorny. Fig. 228. ......
..........................HOLACANTHA, *Holacantha emoryi* **A. Gray**

Figure 228

A small shrubby tree, usually a shrub with greenish bark and minute scale-like leaves that drop early. Yellow flowers grow in dense clusters at the branch tips. They mature into nut-like capsules that open and shed seeds that are relished by burros, goats and rodents.

—ALLTHORN, *Koeberlinia spinosa* Zucc. Similar to Holacantha but more stocky. Flowers are white, in small racemes, have 4 petals and 8 stamens. The fruit is a black berry, tipped with a style and contains 2 seeds.

—CANOTIA, *Canotia holacantha* Torr. is also similar to the two above but has white flowers that grow in axillary racemes and have sepals, petals and stamens in 5's. The fruit is beaked, oblong, woody capsule 1/2"-1" long.

15b Fruiting capsule hairy, leaf lobed. Fig. 229. ....
......CALIFORNIA FREMONTIA, *Fremontia californica* **Torr.**

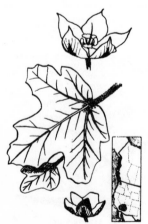

Figure 229

A small tree, up to 20' tall, with wide-spreading branches, grows in dense thickets. The bark is blackish brown, rough and deeply seamed. Young twigs are covered with a rusty down. The leaves are thick, veiny, pubescent and white below. The bright yellow flowers are rose-like, and the hairy fruiting capsule contains reddish brown seeds.

16a Capsule beaked with a persistent style. Fig. 230. ....
PACIFIC RHODODENDRON, *Rhododendron macrophyllum*
....**D. Don**

A small tree, usually a shrub that grows in damp, rich soil of the Pacific coast. Scaly bark covers the lower trunk. The evergreen leaves are clustered at the branch ends. They are green above and lighter or rusty beneath. The clustered flowers have 5 persistent petals. The seed pod develops into a 5-valved capsule with the persistent style forming a beak. Numerous seeds are tufted at the ends. Rhododendrons have some medicinal value, but are said to be poisonous to sheep.

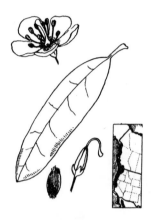

—LILAC, *Syringa japonica* Decne. A tree or shrub that grows up to 30' tall. It has a twisted trunk, fibrous gray bark and pithy twigs. It is planted for its

Figure 230

dark green shiny leaves and large clusters of creamy white flowers. This tree lilac is a native of Japan. Some of the shrubby lilac species are more commonly planted.

16b Pods each contain one seed, tree very thorny. Fig. 231. ....
..................................**SMOKETHORN,** *Dalea spinosa* **A. Gray**

A small tree, up to 18' tall, with a thick trunk and heavy, twisted branches that tend upward. The bark is whitish gray on all the branchlets, twigs and abundant thorns, giving the effect of smoke. On the trunk the bark is deeply seamed, hard, roughened with small scales. Leaves are almost absent. The few that appear are quickly shed. Flowers are deep blue. They mature into beaked pods that each contain 1 kidney-shaped, mottled brown seed. Smokethorn is sometimes planted as an ornamental tree. It is commonly called Smoketree.

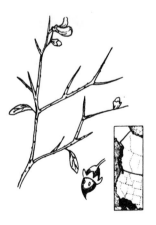

Figure 231

17a Capsule rounded, seeds numerous, leaf margins wavy. Fig. 232. ....TARATA, *Pittosporum eugenioides* A. Cunn.

A small tree, up to 30′ tall with erect, spreading branches and yellow-green leaves with wavy margins. The small flowers are greenish yellow and are clustered near the branch ends. The fruit is a pea-sized capsule with a ridge where the two halves split open. It has been introduced from New Zealand and can be trimmed as a hedge or allowed to grow as a tree.

—TAWHIWHI, *P. tenuifolium* Gaertn. A black barked tree with a 3-valved capsule 1/2″ in diameter and flowers that are purple to black. It is often trimmed as a hedge.

—ORANGE PITTOSPORUM, *P. undulatum* Vent. This tree has leaves that widen near the tip, are dark green and have wavy margins. The 2-valved capsules are 1/2″ in diameter and are brown. The flowers have the fragrance of orange blossoms.

Figure 232

17b Fruit a small capsule, seeds numerous, leaves simple or compound. Fig. 233. LYONTREE, *Lyonothamnus floribundus* A. Gray

A shrub or tree, up to 20′ tall, with clustered stems. The deep reddish brown bark is thin and flaky and often hangs in shreds. Twigs are a shiny red. The fern-like leaves are opposite, evergreen and vary from a simple, entire leaf to a pinnate and doubly pinnate form. They are dark glossy green. Small flowers grow in a flat-topped cyme. The fruits are small, 1/4″ long, woody capsules each containing 4 seeds. The wood is red and very hard, often known as ironwood. It is used for ornamental novelties and the tree itself is planted in gardens because of its attractive foliage.

Figure 233

TREES WITH WINGED SEEDS

1a Seed with long feathery tails 2
1b Seeds not as above 4
2a Leaves deeply lobed. Fig. 234. ....
...................................CLIFFROSE, *Cowania Stanburiana* Torr.

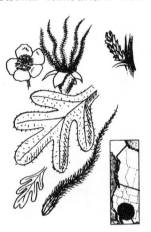

The cliffrose can hardly be called a tree because it is definitely shrub-like, but it grows 15′ tall in favorable locations and is listed as a tree in the checklist. The bark is light colored and shreddy. The leaves are small, deeply lobed and covered with minute glandular specks. The yellow flowers are 5-petaled, rose-like and mature into a seed head with numerous long-tailed achenes. The seeds are oblong and grooved, and the tails are feathery. The cliffrose grows in the arid portions of the southwest and serves as ground cover.

Figure 234

2b Leaves not deeply lobed 3
3a Leaves entire, edges rolled under. Fig. 235. ....
....CURLLEAF CERCOCARPUS, *Cercocarpus ledifolius* Nutt.

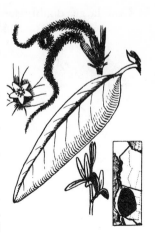

A small tree, up to 25′ tall with a short trunk and crooked, irregular branches forming a rounded crown. The reddish brown bark is hard, firm, thin and scaly. The leaves are dark green above, covered with reddish hair beneath, 1/2″-1″ long, and evergreen lasting 2 seasons. The blades are thick and the leaf edges are strongly curled under. Flowers may be single or clustered and are found in the leaf axils. Flower petals are absent, but the 5 sepals are greenish white. The calyx is woolly. Fruit is a cylindrical, ribbed achene with a long, hairy tail. This tree grows on dry gravelly slopes above 5000′ altitude and provides good ground cover. The wood is fine but cures poorly.

Figure 235

—HAIRY CERCOCARPUS, *C. breviflorus* A. Gray. This is a southwestern species with smaller flowers and leaves that are less curled. These trees were formerly called Mountain Mahoganies.

3b Leaves dentate. Fig. 236. ....

BIRCHLEAF CERCOCARPUS, *Cercocarpus betuloides* **Nutt.**

This tree is similar in size, shape and other characteristics to #3a excepting in the leaf. The dark green leaves are wider, a little longer and dentate beyond the middle. The veins are straight and prominent and the blade is usually flat. They are evergreen.

—ALDERLEAF CERCOCARPUS, *C. b. blancheae* Little is found on the islands of Santa Catalina, and San Cruz. The leaves are less dentate and more oval in shape. They are covered with a dense white wool underneath.

—CATALINA CERCOCARPUS, *C. b. traskiae* Dunkle. A thick-leaved species found on Catalina Island.

Figure 236

4a Fruit a single winged samara. Ashes ....page 145

4b Fruit other than above 5

5a Seeds single, wing circular. ELMS 6

5b Seed a twin with elongate wings. MAPLES 7

6a Leaf large, doubly serrate. Fig. 237. ....

................................AMERICAN ELM, *Ulmus americana* L.

A large, umbrella-shaped tree, up to 125′ tall, with a light gray bark that is rough and ridged. The leaves are dark green, 3″-6″ long, rough and ridged along the veins. The seeds hang in clusters and each seed is entirely surrounded by a thin, fringed wing. An eastern tree, it is commonly planted as a shade tree in the west. Insect pests and diseases are very hard on these trees in some localities and leave them in a ragged condition before the summer is over.

Figure 237

6b Leaf less than half as long, edges serrate. Fig. 238. ....
...................................CHINESE ELM, *Ulmus parvifolia* **Jacq.**

Grows up to 60′ tall, has smooth bark. The dark green leaves are glossy above and are evergreen. Small flowers grow in the leaf axils and mature into small winged seeds. Native of the Orient it is commonly planted in parks, gardens and along avenues. It is fairly drought resistant.

–ENGLISH ELM, *U. campestris* L. with cork-winged branchlets and smaller leaves than the American Elm, is sometimes planted but unpopular because of suckering.

–CORK ELM, *U. thomasi* Sarg. has also been planted on the west coast but is objected to for the same reasons as above.

Figure 238

7a Exceptionally large leaves, edges smooth. Fig. 239. ....
........................BIGLEAF MAPLE, *Acer macrophyllum* **Pursh**

A magnificent shade tree, up to 140′ tall with wide-spreading branches and a dome-shaped crown. The bark is dark brown to black, finely ribbed and often moss-covered. The 5-lobed leaves are large, usually 10″-20″ long, shiny, dark green above, edges entire, lobes pointed. Large drooping clusters of fragrant yellow flowers appear after the leaves in spring. Seeds are abundant covered with bristly hair and having wings that are nearly parallel. This tree is useful as a shade tree and the wood is used for furniture and inside finishing.

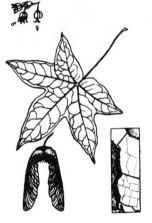

Figure 239

7b Leaves less than 10″ across 8

8a Leaf edges smooth, dentations large. Fig. 240. ....
...................BIGTOOTH MAPLE, *Acer grandidentatum* **Nutt.**

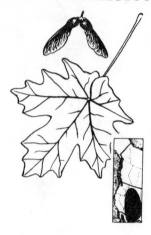

This maple is a bit larger, up to 45′ tall, but otherwise similar to the above in shape. The thin brown bark has plate-like scales. Leaves are dark green, 2″-5″ across, have rounded notches and teeth and turn yellow to scarlet in fall. Cup-like, yellow flowers hang in clusters on long hairy stems. The small rose-colored seeds turn green when mature and are only 1/2″-1″ long. This tree is thinly scattered in its range and grows along mountain streams.

Figure 240

8b Not as above 9

9a Leaf with three main lobes, seed wings wide. Fig. 241. ....
...................ROCKY MOUNTAIN MAPLE, *Acer glabrum* **Torr.**

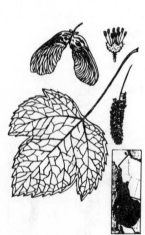

A small tree, up to 30′ tall, often multiple stemmed, with thin, smooth, ashy gray bark and twigs that are bright red in winter. The 3-lobed leaves are bright green, 2″-4″ across and have edges that are finely serrated. The greenish yellow flowers are 10-petaled and appear in clusters of 4-6. Seeds are abundant and are characterized by broad, short wings that form an angle of 90° with each other along the outer edge. Wood from this tree is used locally for repair, tool handles, singletrees and also for fuel.

—DOUGLAS MAPLE, *A. g. douglasii* Dipp. is found in the northern half of the indicated range and is distinguished by leaves that are more leathery, have shorter petioles and lobes that are more widely separated.

Figure 241

9b Leaves with more than 3 lobes 10

10a Leaves 7-9 lobed, samara wings extended. Fig. 242. ....
....VINE MAPLE, *Acer circinatum* Pursh

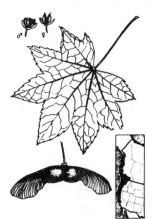

A slender, vine-like tree, up to 20' tall, with smooth, gray-green bark that often has a whitish bloom. The leaves are usually 7-pointed, 1 1/2"-2 1/2" in diameter. Deep red flowers with yellow anthers hang in loose clusters of 10-15. The seeds have wings that are almost at right angles to the stem. This tree is not large enough to find much commercial use, but can be made into tool and implement handles.

Figure 242

10b Leaves not as above 11

11a Leaves 5-lobed 12

11b Leaves divided into leaflets 13

12a Leaves deeply lobed, tips acute. Fig. 243. ....
....SILVER MAPLE, *Acer saccharinum* L.

A large spreading tree, up to 125' tall, with heavy branches and scaly, light gray bark. The deeply 5-lobed leaves are 6"-8" long and silvery white beneath. The flowers are reddish and the winged samara is largest of the maples. An eastern tree, it is commonly grown for shade in the west.

—SUGAR MAPLE, *A. saccharum* Marsh. This common eastern maple has leaves that have acutely pointed lobes. It is very commonly planted as a street tree in its several ornamental varieties.

—JAPANESE MAPLE, *A. palmatum* Thunb. has very deeply lobed leaves. The variety *dissectum* has leaves and seeds that are deep scarlet most of the summer.

Figure 243

12b Leaves not deeply lobed, tips obtuse. Fig. 244. ....
........................SYCAMORE MAPLE, *Acer pseudoplatanus* L.

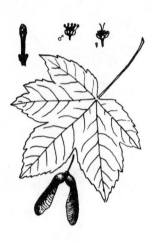

A leafy tree, up to 70′ tall with dark gray, scaly bark. Dark green, shiny leaves are 4″-9″ long, paler beneath. Flowers have noticeably long stamens and hang in long racemes. Seeds are smooth. Native of Europe. Many varieties of this tree are planted.

—NORWAY MAPLE, *A. platanoides* L. Is an European species with tips more acute than the above. Many varieties, including a red-leaved one, are commonly planted in the west.

—RED MAPLE, *A. rubrum* L. A tree with dark green leaves similar to the Norway Maple and flowers and seeds bright scarlet. A very common street maple in the west.

Figure 244

13a Leaflets 3, grows west of the Rockies. Fig. 245. ....
........CALIFORNIA BOXELDER, *Acer negundo californicum*
Sarg.

This variety of boxelder grows in central California and usually has trifoliate leaves.

—INLAND BOXELDER, *A. n. interius* Sarg. This is the variety found east of the Rockies. It is also trifoliate.

—VIOLET BOXELDER, *A. n. violaceum* Jaeg. & Beissn. This variety extends eastward from the boundaries of Washington and Oregon and into the range of *A. n. interius* but can be distinguished from it by thicker leaves that are often entire and pubescent. There may be 3-11 leaflets on one stem and new shoots have a violet-blue bloom on them.

Figure 245

13b Leaflets 3-9, grows east of the Rockies. Fig. 246. ....
....BOXELDER, *Acer negundo* **L.**

A wide-spreading tree up to 75′ tall, with rough, dark gray bark and greenish twigs. Pinnate leaves are compound or double compound, 3-9 leaflets. Male and female flowers on different trees, seeds 1″-2″ long. This fast growing eastern tree is often planted in the west, also some horticultural varieties, such as the Variegated and the dwarf Boxelder.

Figure 246

CACTUS TYPE

1a Stems columnar, ribbed, flowers and fruit at top. Fig. 247. ......
....SAGUARO, *Cereus giganteus* **Engelm.**

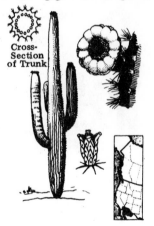

A cactus tree up to 50′ tall with fluted, cylindrical, columnar trunks and branches. Longitudinal ridges carry rows of clustered spines. This tree has no leaves and food manufacturing processes are carried on in the green bark. The white waxy flowers have numerous stamens and grow at the tops of the trunk and branches. These flowers mature into red fruits that split open when ripe. They contain large numbers of seeds. The seeds are ground for oil and the fruit is eaten raw. The fruit is also preserved and used for wine. The structural rods are used for building Indian dwellings and for bows and arrows, also for rustic desert architecture.

Figure 247

ORGANPIPE CACTUS, *C. thurberi* Engelm. Characterized by several vertical stems. Grows abundantly in the Organ Pipe National Monument in Southern Arizona and Northern Mexico.

1b Stems not as above **2**

2a Stems in flattened sections. Fig. 248. ....
....INDIANFIG, *Opuntia ficus-indica* Mill.

Hardly tree-like, but classed as one, up to 13' tall, greatly branched with disc-like joints. The bark is smooth and leathery, varying in color from pale green to yellow-green. Leaves are absent or minute falling readily. Yellow, showy flowers have numerous stamens and a 4-parted pistil. The edible, pear-shaped fruits are full of seeds and covered with small spines. They are used as food. When the spines are singed off the pulpy plant is readily eaten by cattle. Wood rats and other desert rodents are fond of it and eat it in spite of the spines.

Figure 248

—MISSION PRICKLYPEAR, *O. megacantha* Salm. & Dyck. This cactus is similar to Indianfig, but more erect. It was painted around the early missions and ranches and the fruits were used for food. Grows in Southern California.

2b Stems in cylindrical sections. Fig. 249. ....
...........................JUMPING CHOLLA, *Opuntia fulgida* Engelm.

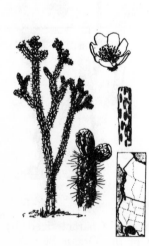

A small, branched tree, up to 15' tall with a stem composed of woody, cylindrical sections. The bark is dark green and is armed with spiral rows of spines. Maroon colored flowers are 2"-3" across. The pulpy pear-shaped fruit is filled with seeds that seldom mature. It propagates by the rooting of fallen joints, hence the name. The dried woody skeleton is used for making various ornamental objects.

—TASAJO, *O. spinosior* Toumey has purple flowers and yellow fruit. It grows in Southern New Mexico and in Arizona.

—STAGHORN CHOLLA, *O. versicolor* Engelm. has greenish yellow flowers tinged with red. The fruit is green. The stems are slender and elongated. Grows in Southern Arizona.

Figure 249

LEAVES USUALLY COMPOUND

1a Leaves palmately compound. The BUCK-
EYES. Fig. 250. 2

Figure 250

1b Leaves pinnately compound.
Fig. 251. 7

Figure 251

2a Leaves tri-foliate 3

2b Leaves with more than three leaflets 6

3a Seed round with thin circular wing, elm-like. Fig. 252. ....
...........NARROWLEAF HOPTREE, *Ptelea angustifolia* **Benth.**

A small shrub or tree, up to 25′ tall, without spines. The bark is smooth and bitter tasting. Trifoliate leaves have long petioles. The flowers are small and greenish white, calyx 4-5 parted. The bitter seed is round, flat and has a gauzy, circular wing similar to that of the elms. This tree grows on rocky slopes, borders of forests and along streams. The bark and roots have medicinal value and the seeds are used as hop in brewing.

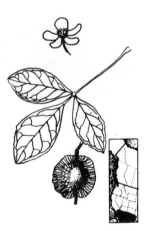

Figure 252

3b Seed other than as above 4

4a Fruit a 3-parted capsule with projecting horns. Fig. 253. ....
............SIERRA BLADDERNUT, *Staphylea bolanderi* A. Gray

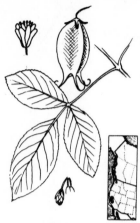

A rather rare shrub or small tree, up to 20' tall. The bark is smooth, sometimes striped. The 3-lobed, finely serrate leaves are 1 1/2"-2 1/2" long and sometimes grow opposite each other. White, perfect flowers form drooping clusters. Each flower has 5 long-clawed petals, a 3-cell ovary and 5 exserted stamens. The fruit is a 3-parted, bladder-like capsule with projecting horns. Each cell contains 1-4 seeds.

Figure 253

4b Fruit not a capsule **5**

5a Fruit a bean pod, seeds bright red ...............................**.....**...........**15**

5b Fruit an ash seed, see p. 145. Fruit a maple seed, see ....p. 123

6a Fruit a pear-shaped husk with one seed inside. Fig. 254. ....
................CALIFORNIA BUCKEYE, *Aesculus californica* Nutt.

A shrubby tree up to 30' tall, with a short, smooth trunk and a flat-topped, open crown. The bark is gray to whitish. Dark green leaflets are 3"-7" long, usually in 5s palmately arranged on a petiole 4"-5" long. Showy, pinkish white flowers grow in erect panicles. The fruit is a pear-shaped husk, 2 1/2"-3" long containing 1 seed that is about 2" in diameter. This tree grows on dry hills and canyon slopes and is useful as ground cover.

—MEXICAN-BUCKEYE, *Ungnadia speciosa* Endel. Barely extends its range into the border states of Texas and New Mexico. Leaves are pinnate instead of palmate with 3-5 leaflets. Flowers are rose-colored. Fruit is 2" in diameter. It is not related to the above.

Figure 254

6b Fruit a rounded, spine covered husk with 3 seeds inside. Fig. 255. ...............HORSECHESTNUT, *Aesculus hippocastanum* **L.**

A symmetrical tree that grows up to 80' tall and has dark brown bark. The palmately compound leaves have 7 leaflets. Erect panicles of showy white flowers develop into rounded spine-covered capsules containing 3 shiny, brown nuts. Several varieties have been developed including one with rose-colored flowers. The tree is native to southern Asia.

Figure 255

9a Husk and nut elongate and smooth. Fig. 256. ....
....PECAN, *Carya illinoensis* **K. Koch**

A heavy-trunked tree, up to 170' tall with light reddish brown bark and woolly twigs with orange lenticels. The leaves are bright yellow-green, petioles yellow. Male flowers in slender catkins, female in 4-angled, tapering spikes. The smooth, reddish, thin-shelled nuts are enclosed in thin, pointed husks and grow in clusters of 3-11. Native of the central states, it is grown commercially in California with limited success, in other parts of the west it is grown as a specimen tree in parks.

Figure 256

9b Nut more rounded **10**

10a Nut wrinkled or grooved **11**

10b Nut nearly smooth, leaflets 15-23. Fig. 257. ....
....HINDS WALNUT, *Juglans hindsii* Jeps.

A large tree, up to 75' tall, with a clear trunk, spreading branches and broad crown. The bark is grayish brown and furrowed. The 15-23 lanceolate, serrate leaflets, 2 1/2"-5" long form a pinnate leaf 10"-15" long. The husk of the fruit is 1 1/2"-2" in diameter and the shelled nut is smooth. This tree is found in only a few locations in central California. The nuts are eaten and the roots used for grafting stock.

Figure 257

11a Nut large, wrinkles rounded, leaflets usually 7. Fig. 258. ....
....ENGLISH WALNUT, *Juglans regia* L.

A spreading tree, up to 80' tall with light gray bark in shallow furrows. Leaves 8"-16" long, green, smooth above and beneath. The fruit is the thin-shelled walnut of commerce. There are many other edible varieties grown, most of them native of Europe and Asia. They are cultivated commercially in Oregon and California.

—BUTTERNUT, *J. cinerea* L. This eastern tree with a sweet oily seed is sometimes cultivated.

Figure 258

11b Leaflets usually 11-23 12

12a Nuts black, heavily wrinkled. Fig. 259. ....
....BLACK WALNUT, *Juglans nigra* **L.**

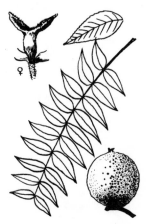

A symmetrical tree up to 150' tall with dark brown, ridged bark. The leaves are 10"-25" long, shiny, bright yellow-green above, hairy beneath. Male flowers in long catkins, female in bi-lobed spike. Fruit a thick-shelled, edible nut. Native of east, widely planted as an ornamental tree in the west.

Figure 259

12b Nuts brown, grooved, tree shrubby. Fig. 260. ....
................CALIFORNIA WALNUT, *Juglans californica* **Wats.**

A more shrubby tree, up to 20' tall, with a short trunk, branches that curve up and then down forming a dome-like crown. Bark on the trunk is blackish brown, deeply furrowed and ridged, to ashy white on young branches. The light yellow-green leaflets are smooth and grow 9-17 on a stem. The fruit is a round, thin-husked, hard-shelled, grooved nut. The wood is used for cabinet work but is not important commercially.

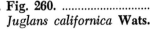

—ARIZONA WALNUT, *J. major* Heller grows in southern Arizona and New Mexico. The nut is thick-shelled, about 1" in diameter and almost smooth.

—LITTLE WALNUT, *J. microcarpa* Berlandier grows in eastern New Mexico and has the smallest nut of any of the Walnuts.

Figure 260

13a Fruit a bean **14**

13b Fruit other than a bean **27**

14a Leaf heart-shaped, blossoms rose-colored. Fig. 261. ....
................CALIFORNIA REDBUD, *Cercis occidentalis* **Torr.**

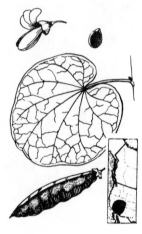

A small tree, up to 12′ tall, with a slender stem and dark brown bark. It usually grows in dense clumps. The leaves are smooth, thick, heart-shaped, with prominent veins and entire edges. Rose colored blossoms come before the leaves in early spring. Seed pods are thin, flat russet brown.

—EASTERN REDBUD, *Cercis canadensis* L. This eastern tree is popular as a park and lawn tree in the northwest for its pink blossoms that come in early spring before the pointed tipped leaves.

Figure 261

14b Leaves pinnate **15**

15a Leaflets 3, beans coral-red. Fig. 262. ....
SOUTHWESTERN CORALBEAN, *Erythrina flabelliformis*
Kearney

A small tree, up to 15′ tall, often with multiple trunks and shrubby. The thin bark is pale, reddish brown, sometimes shreddy. The leaves, usually trifoliate, are oblong and pointed. The pea-like flowers bloom in showy racemes before the leaves appear. Corollas are scarlet, stamens 10. Reddish brown pods, 6″-10″ long, are restricted between the seeds. The beans themselves are a bright coral-red, occasional ones mahogany red, 4-6 in a pod, and about 1/2″ long. This tree grows on sandy desert soil and is useful for stock feed. The seeds, however are narcotic.

Figure 262

15b Leaflets more than 3 16

16a Leaves odd-pinnate 17

16b Leaves even-pinnate 19

17a Leaflets usually 7, pencil-like pods silky white. Fig. 263. ....
.................................MESCALBEAN, *Sophora secundiflora* Lag.

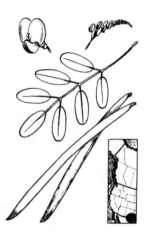

A small, slender tree up to 15' tall, with a narrow crown. The bark is light, grayish brown. The pinnate, oblong leaves persist on the stem till the new ones are ready to form. Fragrant, violet-blue flowers grow in small, one-sided racemes and develop into pencil-like silky white pods that contain up to half a dozen bright scarlet beans. This tree is the coral bean of Texas and grows on light, sandy soil. The seeds are highly narcotic and are used by the Indians in preparing an intoxicating drink.

Figure 263

17b Seed pods brown and flattened, tree thorny 18

18a Flowers rose-colored. Fig. 264. ....
....NEW-MEXICAN LOCUST, *Robinia neo-mexicana* A. Gray

A shrub or tree that grows to be 25' tall with straight trunk and spreading branches. The bark is dark gray to black, hard, with deep furrows and interlacing ridges. Branches and twigs are covered with fine hair and have paired spines. Leaves hairy, pinnate, 4"-10" long, leaflets 1"-1 1/2" long. Fragrant rose-colored blossoms hang in dense racemes. Seed pods are 2"-4" long and hairy.

Figure 264

18b Flowers creamy white. Fig. 265. ....
....................................**BLACK LOCUST,** *Robinia pseudoacacia* **L.**

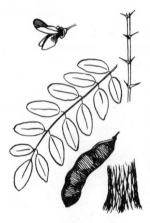

A tree that grows up to 100' tall with a very rough dark brown bark that has interlaced ridges. The dark green leaflets are smooth and entire forming pinnate leaves 8"-14" long. The fragrant, cream colored, pea-like flowers develop into dark brown, flattened pods with 4-8 seeds in each. This eastern tree has been much planted in the west for erosion control on hillsides and also as a roadside tree. From these plantings it has also escaped. It is highly resistant to drought.

Figure 265

19a Seed pods curled in tight spirals when opened. Fig. 266. ......
..........**SCREWBEAN MESQUITE,** *Prosopis pubescens* **Benth.**

A shrubby tree up to 20' tall with many branches. The pale grayish brown bark comes off in loose strips. Twigs have pairs of spines. Leaf stems forked, 1 1/2" long, 5-8 pairs of leaflets on each. Flowers yellowish, in racemes or spikes 2"-3" long. The fruit pods are pale yellow, in clusters of 6-12, cylindrical, 1"-2 1/2" long. When ripe they burst open, scatter their 10-20 small hard seeds and curl up into a tight spiral. The beans are eaten by man and beast. Mexicans grind them to make flour.

Figure 266

19b Seed pods not as above **20**

20a Seed pods flattened and twisted **21**

20b Seed pods not as above **22**

21a Large thorns are often branched. Fig. 267. ....
.................................**HONEYLOCUST,** *Gleditsia triacanthos* **L.**

This large spreading tree, up to 140′ tall, has dark gray bark, branching thorns and beautiful, fernlike foliage. The leaves are pinnate and doubly pinnate, dark green and in graceful sprays. The twisted, flattened, dark russet brown pod contains sweet bean-like seeds. This eastern tree is ornamental but very thorny. Thornless varieties have been developed by grafting.

Figure 267

21b Thorns simple but recurved. Fig. 268. ....
..........................**CATCLAW ACACIA,** *Acacia greggii* **A. Gray**

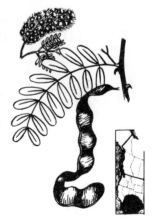

Usually a shrub but sometimes a tree up to 20′ tall with a short trunk and many branches. The twigs have strong recurved thorns that are hard on clothes and skin. The bark is gray to reddish brown. There are 4-8 pairs of leaflets on each division of the branched petiole. Minute yellow flowers with long stamens grow in a dense raceme. Fruiting pods are large, 3″-4″ long, very much twisted and have flat, shiny, deep brown seeds in them. These and a gum from the bark were used by the Indians.

—SWEET ACACIA, *A. farnesiana* Willd. is probably a native of Texas but is now widely cultivated.

Figure 268

—WRIGHT ACACIA, *A. wrightii* Benth. has beans that are shorter and wider than the above. Grows in Southern California and S. W. Texas.

23a Seed pods small, 1/2″ long. Fig. 269. ....
.........................KIDNEYWOOD, *Eysenhardtia polystachya* Sarg.

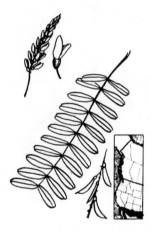

A tree up to 20′ tall with many slender branches. The bark is light gray and has large patch-like scales. Leaves are pinnate with 10-20 pairs of leaflets on a rachis that is 4″-5″ long. The leaflets are pale gray-green and smooth. Creamy white flowers grow in long spike-like clusters. The small beans hang down from the erect stem and curve up. This tree grows on dry gravelly soil.

Figure 269

23b Seed pods longer, tree thornless, flower head ball-like. Fig. 270. ......LITTLELEAF LEADTREE, *Leucaena retusa* Benth.

A small tree that grows up to 25′ tall and has reddish brown bark. The young twigs are covered with a whitish powder. The tree is without thorns. The leaves are similar to the acacias, have branched petioles and form feathery sprays. The white flowers grow in dense, globose heads 3/4″ in diameter. Each flower has 10 stamens. The fruiting pod is smooth, flattened, sometimes restricted between seeds, dark reddish brown with seeds still darker. These trees grow on steep rocky hillsides of the interior southwestern deserts.

Figure 270

24a Leaflets small, 4-6 on a petiole, Fig. 271. ....
.....................BLUE PALOVERDE, *Circidium floridum* **Benth.**

A short-trunked tree, up to 25' tall, with many heavy branches that are gnarled and usually almost leafless. Twigs are spiny. The bark is smooth, light, yellowish green except near the base where it turns to light brown. Photosynthesis takes place in the small yellow-green twigs. Leaves are similar to the acacias but small, sparse and early deciduous. Yellow flowers form clusters. The beans are 2"-4" long and contain 3-8 seeds. The wood is suitable for fuel but is easily consumed because it is light and often punky.

—YELLOW PALOVERDE, *C. microphyllum* Rose & Johnst. Has smaller leaves, cylindrical pods and a more bronzy green bark. Found from Southern California to New Mexico.

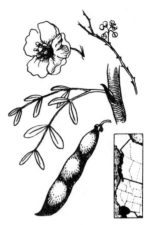

Figure 271

24b Leaflets more numerous 25

25a Flowers yellowish 26

25b Flowers purplish, thorns short and recurved. Fig. 272. ....
....TESOTA, *Olneya tesota* **A. Gray**

A small tree, up to 20' tall, with a short, thick trunk and a crown of thick, upright limbs and thorny twigs. The deep, reddish brown bark is flaky and sheds easily. Leaves are pinnate with 6-10 leaflets on each rachis. They remain on the tree till after the new ones come on in spring. The small, purplish pea blossoms grow in short cymes and develop into light, russet-brown pods containing 2-4 seeds. These seeds are flat, oval, shiny, brown and hard. They are roasted and eaten by desert dwellers and are said to taste like peanuts. The wood of this tree is extremely hard and heavy and finds use as a fuel. The tree is commonly called Desert Ironwood.

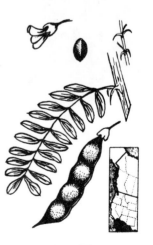

Figure 272

26a Leaflets minute, 20-50 pairs, bark reddish. Fig. 273. ....
.......................JERUSALEM-THORN, *Parkinsonia aculeata* **L.**

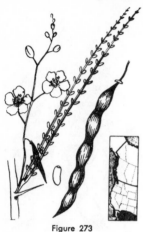

Figure 273

A tree that grows up to 25′ tall and has a short trunk and drooping branches. The thin bark is reddish brown and the twigs have heavy thorns. The identifying feature is the long, 6″-18″, forked rachis with from 10-50 pairs of small scale-like leaflets. The yellow flowers are 3/4″-1″ in diameter and form loose racemes. Pods are 2″-6″ long, yellow-brown, restricted between the 4-8 seeds. The tree is sometimes planted as an ornamental species because of its unusual leaf form.

26b Bark gray, leaflets 15-20 pairs. Fig. 274. ....
....MESQUITE, *Prosopis juliflora* **DC.**

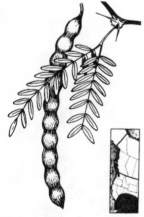

Figure 274

A small tree, up to 40′ tall, with a slender trunk, but an enormous root system and a long, heavy taproot, that goes down to water. The bark is rough, ashy gray on the trunk, reddish on the branches. About 15-20 pairs of leaflets grow on each division of the branched leaf stem. These petioles are enlarged and glandular at the base. The yellow-green flowers grow in spikes 2″-3 1/2″ long. Fruit pods are 4″-8″ long, flattened when green, but swelled at the seeds as they mature. They are usually straight, but sometimes curved. Mexicans and Indians make sun-baked cakes from the ground pods. The seeds have a sweet gum in them that dissolves readily in water.

—TORREY MESQUITE, *P. j. torreyana* L. Benson is a more eastern variety.

27a Fruit berry-like **28**

27b Fruit a winged seed **34**

28a Fruit in upright clusters, SUMACS **29**

28b Fruit not as above **30**

29a Leaves usually simple, fruit clusters small. Fig. 275. ....
......**MAHOGANY SUMAC,** *Rhus integrifolia* **Benth. & Hook.**

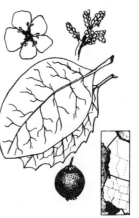

A small slender tree, up to 20′ tall with an open irregular crown. The bark is gray to clear red-brown on the twigs. The evergreen leaves are thick, usually single, sometimes trifoliate, entire or dentate. Flower clusters are small and loose. Fruit is covered with a red down. –SUGAR SUMAC, *R. ovata* S. Wats. is similar to the above but has shiny leaves and berries covered with a sweet wax. Found in Arizona and California.

Figure 275

29b Leaves compound, fruit clusters larger. Fig. 276. ....
....**SMOOTH SUMAC,** *Rhus glabra* **L.**

A small, slender tree, up to 15′ tall with heavy twigs. The bark is smooth, greenish brown. Serrate leaflets, 2″-3″ long, turn deep scarlet in fall. The male flowers are small and white and form branched clusters, the female are ball-like and form heavy branched clusters that mature into pyramidal, dense masses of red berries. A beverage is made of the berries which have a high tannin content. The tree is sometimes used for ornamental purposes because of the attractive foliage, especially in fall.

Figure 276

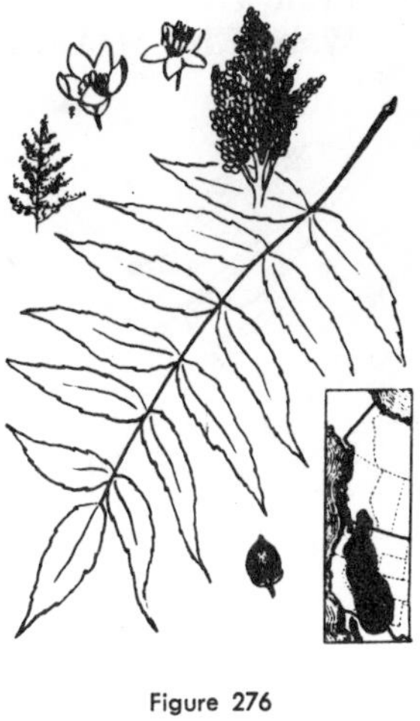

–KEARNEY SUMAC, *R. kearneyi* Barkley is found in the central southwest.
–LAUREL SUMAC, *R. laurina* Nutt. has abundant, aromatic leaves and a dense panicle of flowers. Berries are small and whitish. Grows in Southern California.

—LITTLELEAF SUMAC, *R. microphylla* Engelm. has considerably smaller leaves. Found in West Texas, New Mexico and Arizona.

30a Trunk and branches unusually swollen, sap and fruit red. Fig. 277. ....**ELEPHANTTREE,** *Bursera microphylla* **A. Gray**

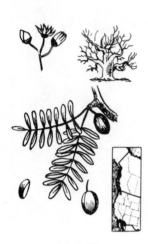

A small, short-trunked tree, up to 20′ tall, with many fat branches forming a rounded head. The bark is pale yellow, paper-thin and scaly. Cuts produce a blood-red sap. The pinnate leaves grow in sparse clusters, are 1″-1 1/2″ long and have 5-17 minute leaflets. The 5-petaled, white flowers are about 1/4″ long, usually in 3-flowered clusters and numerous. Berries are red, 3-sided and contain triangular seeds. This tree grows on hard sterile soil and is rare in United States, but more plentiful south of the border.

—FRAGRANT BURSERA, *B. fagaroides* Engler is found in southern Arizona and adjacent Mexico. It is characterized by its sweet odor.

Figure 277

30b Trunk not as above, fruit in drooping clusters **31**

31a Fruit a yellow berry, in clusters. Fig. 278. ....
WESTERN SOAPBERRY, *Sapindus drummondii* **Hook. & Arn.**

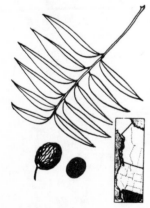

A tree, up to 60′ tall with erect, twisted branches and a buttressed base. The bark is gray, rough and scaly, twigs are yellow-green, have lenticels showing. Odd pinnate leaves with 9-17 leaflets that are smooth above and woolly beneath. The flowers are white in panicles 6″-9″ long. Yellow fruit ripens later and remains on the tree through the winter, contains one dark brown seed.

Figure 278

31b Fruit not a yellow berry **32**

32a Fruit blue, in dense clusters, twigs pithy. Fig. 279. ....
...........................BLUEBERRY ELDER *Sambucus glauca* **Nutt.**

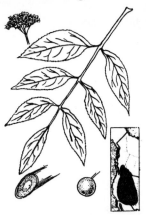

Usually a tall shrub, but also a tree form, up to 20' tall, with a dense round crown and many erect stems. The dark, yellowish brown bark has deep, connected ridges, but is thin and shiny, reddish brown on the twigs, often covered with whitish bloom. The smooth, medium green leaves are lighter below and have 3-9 leaflets. White to yellow flowers grow in large flat-topped cymes. These mature into large clusters of blue-black berries covered with a whitish bloom. They have a strongly flavored pulp, used in jellies, and contain 1-3 seeds. The fruit is eaten by birds. Wood from this tree is soft and brittle and finds no commercial use.

Figure 279

—MEXICAN ELDER, *S. mexicana* Presl. grows in the southern limits of the area marked on the map.

—BLACKBEAD ELDER, *S. melanocarpa* A. Gray. This black elder grows in the mountains from Arizona north to the Canadian border.

—VELVET ELDER, *S. velutina* Durand & Hilgard is found in Arizona and California. It has downy leaves and pale yellow flowers.

32b Fruit red 33

33a Leaflets 5-7, twigs pithy. Fig. 280. ....
............PACIFIC RED ELDER, *Sambucus callicarpa* **Greene**

A shrub or small tree, up to 30' tall, with slender branchlets and thin, scaly, light brown bark. The leaves are 6"-10" long and have 5-7 dark green leaflets. White or yellowish flowers form large cymes, 2 1/2"-3" in diameter. The bright red berries are about 1/4" in diameter. These berries find some medicinal use and are also used for flavoring preserves. The wood is used for little other than pop guns and whistles. It grows in the moist, rich soil along river banks.

Figure 280

34a Leaflets small and narrow, berries in loose panicle. Fig. 281.
....................CALIFORNIA PEPPERTREE, *Schinus molle* L.

A wide-spreading tree, up to 50′ tall, with a dark brownish bark. Leaves are made up of 20-60 light green, shiny leaflets. Creamy white flowers grow in large, loose clusters at branch ends. These mature into pea-sized reddish berries. A native of Peru, this tree is widely planted in southern California and Arizona.

Figure 281

34b Leaflets broader, berries vermilion in dense clusters. Fig. 282.
..............EUROPEAN MOUNTAINASH, *Sorbus aucuparia* L.

A slender tree, up to 50′ tall with a thin, gray bark. There are usually 9-15 dark green leaflets in 1 leaf 5″-10″ long. White flowers bloom in a cyme 5″ wide and develop into a dense cluster of bright red berries that remain on the tree all winter. A native of Europe it is widely planted as an ornamental lawn tree in the west and attracts birds in winter.

—SITKA MOUNTAIN ASH, *Sorbus sitchensis* usually a shrub, sometimes reaches tree size.

Figure 282

35a Seed wing broad, leaves simple or trifoliate. Fig. 283. ....
...........................SINGLELEAF ASH, *Fraxinus anomala* **Torr.**

A small tree, up to 30' tall, with bark that is gray and has small, hard ridges. The leaves are usually single, but sometimes have 2-3 leaflets. They are dark green above, paler and hairy beneath, 1 1/2"-2" long and proportionately broader than most ashes. Cup-shaped flowers appear in clusters in the leaf axils on new twigs and have orange anthers. The seeds are short, 1/2" long, and have broad wings. This tree grows along streams but is never very plentiful.

–LOWELL ASH, *F. a. lowellii* Little. This ash is similar to the Gregg Ash, but has longer leaves, no webs on the rachis, a flatter seed and a broader wing.

Figure 283

35b Leaflets more numerous 36

36a Leaflets small, 1/2"-3/4" long, seed large. Fig. 284. ....
....GREGG ASH, *Fraxinus greggii* **A. Gray**

A small tree, up to 25' tall, often shrub-like with gray to light brown bark. The small leaves are 1 1/2"-3" long and have webbed petioles. Dark green leaflets, 3-7 in number are 1/2"-3/4" long. The cup-shaped flowers are perfect, 1/2"-3/4" and have 1-2 stamens. Fruits are small, about 1/2" long and have a short, round seed.

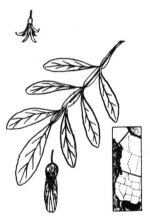

–TWO-PETAL ASH, *F. dipetala* Hook. & Arn. This ash with a 2-petal flower is found from central California south to the border.

Figure 284

36b Leaflets and seeds not as above **37**

37a Leaflets 7 on one petiole, seeds slender. Fig. 285. ....
....WHITE ASH, *Fraxinus americana* L.

A tree up to 120′ tall with a dark brown bark that is deeply fissured. Leaflets are dark green above and lighter below. Dark purple flowers mature into large clusters of winged seeds 1″-2″ long. This tree is a native of the eastern states and is planted in parks and gardens in the west.

—GREEN ASH, *F. pennsylvanica* Marsh. This eastern tree with usually 7 leaflets and small seeds is also often planted in the west.

Figure 285

37b Leaflets 5, native of the western states **38**

38a Leaflets sessile or subsessile. Fig. 286. ....
.....................................OREGON ASH, *Fraxinus latifolia* Benth.

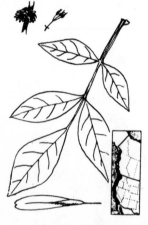

A tree that grows up to 70′ tall, has a long, clean trunk and a short narrow crown. The thick, soft bark is dull gray to brown and has wide ridges. Leaves are thick, yellow-green, 6″-12″ long and have 5-7 leaflets 3″-6″ long. Male and female flowers appear on different trees about the time the leaves come out. Seeds 1 1/2″-2″ long hang in heavy clusters. The wood is used for tool handles and implements.

Figure 286

38b Leaflets not sessile **39**

39a Petiole and rachis covered with fine hair. Fig. 287. ....
....**VELVET ASH,** *Fraxinus velutina* **Torr.**

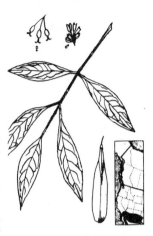

A slender, short-trunked tree up to 30′ tall with bark that is soft, scaly, broad-ridged and reddish gray in color. Leaves are 4″-6″ long and have fine hair on the rachis. The 3-9 smooth, thick leaflets are deep yellow-green, lighter beneath. Fruit forms thick clusters.

—LEATHERLEAF ASH, *F. v. coreacea* Rehd. Differs from the species in having a more leathery leaf that is also considerably broader.

—SMOOTH ASH, *F. v. glabra* Rehd. is found in Arizona, New Mexico, Texas.
—TOUMEY ASH, *F. v. toumeyi* Rehd. grows in southern Arizona and New Mexico.

Figure 287

—FRAGRANT ASH, *F. cuspidata* Torr. has narrow leaves and very fragrant flowers. Grows in Texas and New Mexico.

F. c. macropetal Rehd. has larger, simple leaves at the base of the branchlets.

39b Seed not the ash type **40**

40a Seed in the middle of the wing. Fig. 288. ....
....**AILANTHUS,** *Ailanthus altissima* **Swingle**

A fast growing tree, up to 100′ tall with thin, rough, gray bark and green twigs. Leaflets, 13-41 on a leaf, have an unpleasant odor. Yellow-green flowers in large clusters also emit foul odor. The fruit is a propeller-like wing with a seed in the center. The tree is a native of China. In spite of its foul odor and ability to become a weed it is commonly called Tree-of-Heaven. It has escaped from cultivation in central California.

Figure 288

40b Leaves doubly branched, fern-like. Fig. 289. ....
....SILK-OAK, *Grevilla robusta* Cunn.

An evergreen tree, up to 70' tall and more, with fern-like leaves. The orange flowers have long styles and grow in abundance on 1-sided racemes 2"-4" long, developing into follicles containing 2 flat, winged seeds each. This Australian tree grows rapidly in a hot, dry habitat and is frequently planted in parks and gardens of southern California.

—SILVER TREE, *Leucadendron argenteum* R. Br. A small tree, native of South Africa, with hairy lanceolate leaves that are silvery white on both sides. Its fruit is small, a nut with persistent style.

Figure 289

LIST OF TREES ACCORDING TO THEIR ORDERS AND FAMILIES

A N attempt has been made in this list to follow the sequence in most common use, but since taxonomists do not always agree on the order or the names of the orders and families it is not possible for this list to be an undisputed standard. It will be useful for the information it gives on relationship of the various trees and also as a check list.

GYMNOSPERMS

ORDER GINKGOALES

1. GINKOECEAE, *Ginkgo* Family

1. Genus *Ginkgo*

ORDER CONIFERALES

1. PINACEAE, Pine Family

1. Genus *Pinus*, The Pines

149

2. Genus *Larix*, The Larches

3. Genus *Picea*, The Spruces

4. Genus *Tsuga*, The Hemlocks

5. Genus *Pseudotsuga*, The False Hemlocks

6. Genus *Abies*, The Firs

3. Genus *Juniperus*, The Junipers

4. Genus *Libocedrus*, The Incense-Cedars

5. Genus *Thuja*, The Arborvitaes

6. Genus *Thujopsis*

ANGIOSPERMS

ORDER PALMALES

1. PALMACEAE, Palm Family

1. Genus *Washingtonia*, The Washington Palms

2. Genus *Trachycarpus*

3. Genus *Sabal*, The Cabbage Palms

4. Genus *Phoenix*, The Date Palms

5. Genus *Cocos*, The Cocos Palms

ORDER LILIALES

1. LILIACEAE, Lily Family

1. Genus *Yucca*, The Yuccas

2. Genus *Cordyline*, The Dracenas

3. Genus *Dracaena*, The Dracenas

ORDER SCITAMINALES

1. MUSACEAE, Banana Family

1. Genus *Musa*, The Bananas

ORDER SALICALES

1. SALICACEAE, Willow Family

1. Genus *Populus*, The Poplars

2. Genus *Salix*, The Willows

ORDER GARRYALES

1. GARRYACEAE, Garrya Family

1. Genus *Garrya*

ORDER MYRICALES

1. MYRICACEAE, Waxmyrtle Family

1. Genus *Myrica*, The Waxmyrtles

ORDER JUGLANDALES

1. JUGLANDACEAE, Walnut Family

1. Genus *Juglans*, The Walnuts

2. Genus *Carya*, The Hickories

ORDER FAGALES

1. BETULACEAE, Birch Family

1. Genus *Betula*, The Birches

2. Genus *Alnus*, The Alders

3. Genus *Ostrya*, The Hophornbeams

3. Genus *Amelanchier*, The Serviceberries

4. Genus *Photinia*, The Christmasberries

5. Genus *Malus*, The Apples

6. Genus *Pyrus*, The Pears

7. Genus *Cydonia*, The Quinces

8. Genus *Cowania*, The Cliffroses

9. Genus *Prunus*, The Prunes and Cherries

10. Genus *Vauquelinia*

11. Genus *Sorbus*, The Mountain-Ashes

6. LEGUMINOSAE, Legume Family

1. Genus *Cercis*, The Redbuds

2. Genus *Gleditsia*, The Honeylocusts

3. Genus *Robinia*, The Locusts

4. Genus *Sophora*

5. Genus *Erythrina*

6. Genus *Prosopis*, The Mesquites

7. Genus *Acacia*, The Acacias

8. Genus *Olneya*

9. Genus *Eysenhardtia*

10. Genus *Cercidium*

ORDER PARIETALES

1. TAMARICACEAE, Tamarisk Family

1. Genus *Tamarix*

2. KOEBERLINIACEAE, Koeberline Family

1. Genus *Koeberlinia*

3. BIGNONIACEAE, Bignonia Family

1. Genus *Chilopsis*

2. Genus *Paulownia*

3. Genus *Catalpa*

ORDER OPUNTIALES

1. CACTACEAE, Cactus Family

1. Genus *Cereus*

2. Genus *Opuntia*, The Pricklypears

ORDER MYRTALES

1. ELAEAGNACEAE, Oleaster Family

1. Genus *Shepherdia*

2. Genus *Eleagnus*

2. PUNICACEAE, Pomegranate Family

1. Genus *Punica*

3. MYRTACEAE, Myrtle Family

2. Genus *Eucalyptus,* The Gums

3. Genus *Melaleuca*

4. Genus *Callistemon*

ORDER UMBELLALES

1. CORNACEAE, Dogwood Family

1. Genus *Cornus,* The Dogwoods

ORDER ERICALES

1. ERICACEAE, Heath Family

1. Genus *Rhododendron*

2. Genus *Arbutus*, The Madrones

ORDER EBENALES

1. SAPOTACEAE, Sapodilla Family

1. Genus *Bumelia*

2. EBENACEAE, Ebony Family

1. Genus *Diospyros*, The Persimmons

ORDER OLEALES

1. OLEACEAE, Olive Family

1. Genus *Fraxinus*, The Ashes

2. Genus *Olea*, The Olives

3. Genus *Syringa*

ORDER RUBIALES

1. RUBIACEAE, Madder Family

1. Genus *Cephalanthus*

2. CAPRIFOLIACEAE, Honeysuckle Family

1. Genus *Sambucus,* The Elderberries

INDEX AND PICTURED GLOSSARY

The scientific names are italicized, the common names are not. Family names and glossary words are all in capitals.

Fig. 290

Fig. 291

Fig. 292

Fig. 293

D

N

NODE: a joint where buds occur, Fig. 294; 6

Node

Fig. 294

O

OBLANCEOLATE: tapered toward the stem, 4
OBLONG: longer than broad, sides roughly parallel, 4
OBTUSE: point greater than a right angle, 6
OVARY: enlarged part of the pistil containing the ovules, Fig. 295; 9
OVULE: the immature seed, Fig. 295; 9

Ovule Ovary

Fig. 295

P

PALMATE: radiating, as fingers do on a hand, Fig. 296; 5

Fig. 296

PANICLE: a loose cluster as in oat, 8
PARTED: lobes cleft to the point of separation, 6

Fig. 297

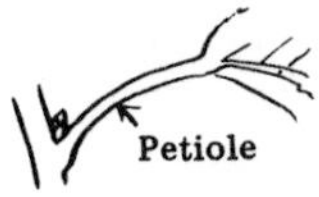

Fig. 298

Fig. 299

Fig. 300

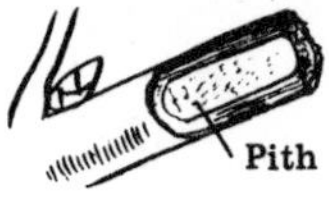

Fig. 301

Fig. 302

Fig. 303